A Guide to
OLD KONA

Kona Historical Society
Kalukalu, Hawai'i

ISBN 0–8248–2010–X

FINANCIAL SUPPORT PROVIDED BY:
State Foundation on Culture and the Arts
State Department of Business, Economic Development and Tourism
Hawaii Electric Foundation
Caroline Shipman Foundation

Dedication

This guidebook is dedicated to the memory of the following people, all former supporters of the Kona Historical Society. They are missed.

Jock Ackerman
Lindsey Child
Cornelia Crumpacker
Francis Cushingham
Frances Cushingham
Yosoto Egami
Rose Falconer
Jack Fitzgibbons
Rose Fujimori
Amy Greenwell
Alice Greenwell
Beatrice Greenwell
Henry Greenwell
Jack Greenwell
Norman Greenwell
Robert Greenwell
Robert Hind
Mona Holmes
Red Hunt
Richard Ishida
Robert Judd
Martha Judd

Ha'i Kamakau
Mahone Ka'eo
Sam Liau
Erma Lillie
Robert Lowrey
Dr. Tom Mar
Loy Marks
Hana Masuhara
Dr. Kid McCoy
Nona McCoy
Dorothy Mitchell
Rikio Morimoto
Chiyoku Nakamaru
Buzz Newman
Irvine Paris
Robert Paris
Sybil Paris
Kathy Pearson
Howard Pierce
Johnny Rapoza
Willie Rapoza

Beth Richards
Fred Richards
Marjorie Robertson
Bob Rogers
Adrian Saxe
Thelma Springer
Pilipo Springer
Alfred Smith
Arthur Takahara
Willy Thompson
Barbara Thurston
Lorrin Thurston
Marguerite Vanderbilt
Alice Wall
Roy Wall
Harvey Weeks
Helen Weeks
John Weeks
Marge Weinrich
Gwen Williams
Roger Williams

Contents

Contents

Cattle shipping at Nāpo'opo'o Beach, Kealakekua Bay, ca. 1925.
(Courtesy Barbara Fitzgibbons Collection, KHS Archives)

* Site designated as a National Historic Landmark.
† Site listed on the National Register of Historic Places.

Preface

It would be impossible to include all of Kona's historic sites in this book. Therefore, only sites that are easily accessible to the public or illustrative of important aspects of Kona's history have been selected for description. If a site is not open to the public, it will be noted in the site description.

The site descriptions are meant to offer only a bit of an introduction to the history of the area. It is our hope that readers interested in learning more will visit Kona Historical Society's library and archive to do further research. At the end of each site description are numbers in parentheses. The first number refers to a specific title in the bibliography at the back of this book, and the second is the page number in that book.

A timeline of both international and Hawaiian historical events can also be found at the back of this guide. Each of the site descriptions includes a symbol that corresponds to a specific time period in the Hawai'i timeline. Using these symbols as a guide, the reader can fit Kona's historic sites into the larger framework of Hawaiian history.

The petroglyph ⚶ is Hawai'i at the time of Polynesian discovery.
The feathered helmet ⬤ is Kamehameha I's lifetime.
The crown ⬤ represents the Hawaiian monarchy established by Kamehameha I and lasting until Queen Lili'uokalani's overthrow in 1893.
The crossed rifles ✕ represent the end of the Hawaiian monarchy.
The American flag ⬛ marks Hawai'i's annexation to the United States as a territory in 1898 and as a state in 1959.

Acknowledgments

This guidebook represents a community effort involving the input and research of many volunteers and the Kona Historical Society staff. The late Pilipo Springer, Megan Mitchell, and David Bucy & Associates helped with the general concept of the book. Maps were done by Aaron Shimakura and Lucie Aono of the University of Hawai'i Press provided her publishing expertise.

Maile Melrose has been our principal writer. Initial editing was done by Jean Greenwell, Sheree Chase, and other members of the Kona Historical Society staff.

We are grateful to many other members of our community who took time to contribute to this project: Fanny AuHoy, Dorothy Barrere, Roland Crisafi, Sherwood Greenwell, Alfreida Fujita, Herb Kane, Shoji Kawahara, Take Kudo, Eugene Leslie, Ruby McDonald, Holly McEldowney, Clarence Medeiros, Art Murata, Sachie Murata, Buddy Norwood, Diana Nui, William Paris, David Roy, Ichiro Shikada, Julia Soehren, Lloyd Soehren, Hannah Springer, Marie Strazar, Allen Wall, Cheeta Wilson, and Terry Wallace.

This guidebook is a first attempt for the Kona Historical Society. As such, it probably will be revised in the future, so suggestions and corrections are welcomed.

JILL OLSON, Project Director &
Executive Director of Kona Historical Society

Kalukalu, Hawai'i, June 1997

Introduction

Welcome to Kona, a beautiful and historic part of the island of Hawai'i, the largest of the Hawaiian Islands. Despite modern hotels and bustling shopping centers, Kona is a rural district at heart, known for its calm seas, balmy weather, and productive agricultural lands.

The Polynesians who first settled the Kona district found this area to be rich and fruitful. They discovered offshore waters teeming with fish, fertile pockets of soil for gardens, protected bays and inlets ideal for man-made fishponds, glassy waves for surfing and swimming, and an unbeatable climate for year-round living.

Those first migrants, ancestors of present day Hawaiians, accomplished the remarkable feat of transplanting an entire culture by canoe from one small island to another, across thousands of miles of

Kahuwai Bay, Ka'ūpūlehu, North Kona, ca. 1912. Native grass houses at the bay. (Courtesy Maquire Stillman & Springer Collection, KHS Archives)

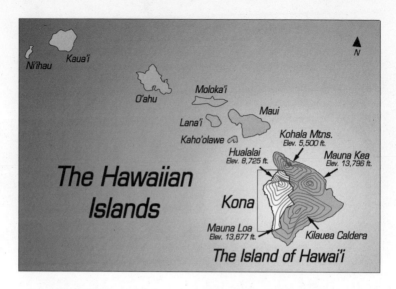

The Hawaiian Islands

The Island of Hawai'i

Map of Kona

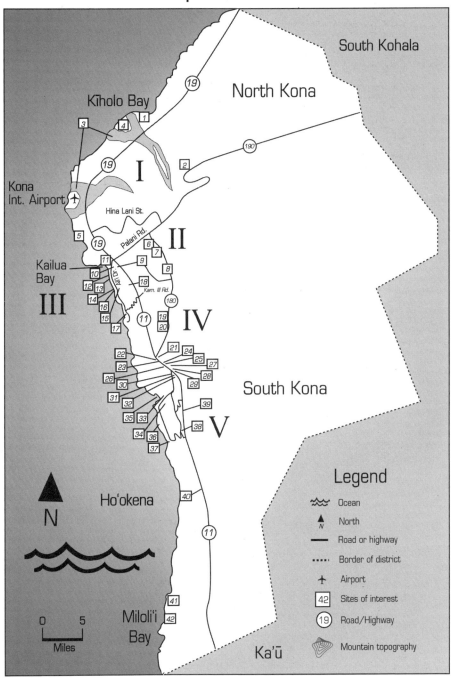

South Kohala

North Kona

Kīholo Bay

I

Kona
Int. Airport

Hina Lani St.

Palani Rd.

II

Kailua
Bay

III

Kam. III Rd.

IV

South Kona

V

Ho'okena

N

Miloli'i
Bay

Ka'ū

Legend

- ～～ Ocean
- ▲ North
- — Road or highway
- ····· Border of district
- ✈ Airport
- 42 Sites of interest
- 19 Road/Highway
- Mountain topography

0 5
Miles

open ocean. Bringing the food plants they needed to survive, they transformed Hawai'i into a Polynesian garden. Surviving examples of their stone *heiau* (temples), house platforms, *pu'uhonua* (places of refuge), and major walls are treasured reminders of Kona's past.

Kona was not without problems. A shortage of fresh water challenged its first residents, just as it does today. Unlike the windward side of Hawai'i, where waterfalls pour into the sea, Kona has no permanent streams or pools. This factor always has limited growth on this leeward side of the island and droughts have shriveled crops and countryside for centuries. Hawaiians learned to flourish in this environment by perfecting dryland farming techniques and conserving limited supplies of spring water.

Active volcanoes also threatened life and property in old Hawai'i. This island boasts the tallest volcano, Mauna Kea (13,796 feet), the largest volcano, Mauna Loa (13,677 feet), and the most active volcano, Kīlauea (4,093 feet), on planet Earth. Plus, Kona has

Kamehameha I, ca. 1816, by artist Louis Choris. (Courtesy Bishop Museum Archives)

Hualālai, its own active volcano, looming 8,271 feet above Kailua village. These mighty mountains shield Kona from blustery tradewinds and create the special climate Kona enjoys. However, since 1983, the continuing eruption at Kīlauea sometimes fills Kona's formerly crystal clear skies with volcanic pollution, otherwise known as vog.

Surrounded by lofty peaks, Kona's important directions are uphill and downhill. Two Hawaiian words express local geography best: *mauka* (toward the mountains) and *makai* (toward the sea). These terms help when navigating Kona's winding roads and sloping terrain. They also illustrate the mountains-to-the-sea orientation of the traditional Hawaiian way of life in which land was divided into strips that included off-shore waters and reefs, shoreline, inland farmland, rainforest, and, perhaps, the summit of a mountain. Hawaiians called these wedges of land *ahupua'a*. Within these *ahupua'a*, most items necessary to sustain life could be either found, grown or harvested. The names of *ahupua'a* persist in Kona and appear on street signs, public buildings, and local maps.

For the visitor interested in history, Kona is a gold mine. Nowhere else in Hawai'i did so much political, social, and religious change happen in so short a time and with such major consequences.

First, Captain James Cook experienced honor and then unexpected death at Kealakekua Bay in 1779. Fifteen years later, Captain George Vancouver unloaded cattle and sheep for Kona's new ruling chief, Kamehameha, near the same rocks where Cook had fallen. Using Western guns and ships to conquer his enemies, Kamehameha waged almost continuous war to become king of the

The Kona District from Kailua Bay looking at Hualālai, 1934. Note inked-in line—indicates Coffee Belt on the Government Road. (Courtesy College of Tropical Agriculture, KHS Archives)

Hawaiian Islands and earn his place in history as Kamehameha the Great. By the time he died in Kailua in 1819, he had seen his people catapulted from the Stone Age into the 19th century.

Weeks after his death, Kamehameha's wives and son, Liholiho, instigated the overthrow of the ancient Hawaiian religion. Fighting to uphold the old gods, Chief Kekuaokalani and his wife Manono died at Kuamoʻo near Keauhou Bay. In 1820, American Protestant missionaries first set foot on Hawaiian soil in Kailua and introduced ideas that would profoundly affect all Hawaiʻi and its people.

It was a missionary, Samuel Ruggles, who first planted coffee in Kona in 1828. Through good times and bad, coffee survived to play an important role in Kona's economy. Attempts to grow large crops of cotton, tobacco, pineapples, sugar, and oranges met obstacles and eventually failed. The tall spikes of sisal now growing wild along Palani Road are a reminder that 20,000 sisal plants were imported to Kona from Florida in 1893. A sisal mill was established not far from

Hawaiian woman with flowering coffee branch, 1934. (Courtesy University of Hawaiʻi Agricultural Experiment Station Collection, KHS Archives)

Kailua. With the passing of sailing ships, this fledgling fiber industry died, like so many other brave attempts at diversified agriculture.

The word "independent" is often used to describe Kona residents. Tales are told recounting the ordeals of 19th century immigrants who fled to Kona to escape harsh conditions on sugar plantations in Hilo, Puna, and Hāmākua. As illegal runaways, the fugitives traveled by night, hiding in bushes by day, carrying their few possessions on their backs as they fled to freedom. Once they reached Kona, they changed their names to escape detection. As coffee farmers, fishermen, pedlars, and carpenters, they built new identities for themselves in a district where people asked few questions.

Hawai'i, the most remote island chain on Earth, was settled and transformed by the Polynesians over one thousand years ago. During the past 200 years, this process of change and growth has continued as new waves of immigrants have arrived. New settlers have brought traditions and customs from their own homelands which continue to change Kona. Today, Kona is a multi-cultural community that takes pride in its ethnic diversity, its unusual history, and its promising future.

We hope that your travels will be fruitful and fun, and that *A Guide to Old Kona* will inspire an appreciation of the interesting people, places, and events that have shaped Kona's history. In addition, as you wander *mauka* to *makai*, take the time to enjoy Kona's beauty. As the Hawaiians of old used to say:

Pili aloha o Kona, ho'oipo i ka malie.

Love remains close to Kona, who woos the calm.

1. Kīholo

At the close of the 20th century, Kīholo remains a green oasis along a stark and blackened coast. Threatened and then almost completely destroyed by volcanic eruptions in the past century, little remains today of the once important settlement.

In 1801, the village of Kīholo escaped destruction when lava from nearby Hualālai entered the sea just south of Kīholo's famous fishpond. A jet black river of basalt, clearly visible nearly 200 years later (park at the scenic overlook at the 82 mile marker on Queen Ka'ahumanu Highway, Hwy.19), illustrates that historic lucky break.

North Kona

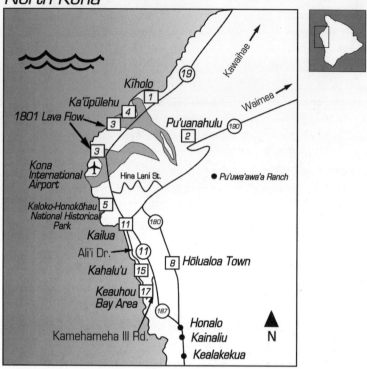

In 1859, however, Kīholo was not so fortunate. A flood of lava from Mauna Loa, visible today on the northern edge of the bay, transformed Kīholo from a former residence of chiefs to a sparsely populated fishing village.

Once the site of one of Kona's largest fishponds, Kīholo played an important role in the success of Kamehameha the Great's armies. Vast numbers of coastal mullet were harvested at Kīholo fishpond to feed his warriors. Without this dependable food supply, his ambitious plans to conquer the entire island of Hawai'i and, later, all the Hawaiian Islands, might have failed.

Before Kamehameha returned to Kona in 1812, after living with his court on O'ahu for several years, he gave orders to have the fishpond at Kīholo repaired. It took the labor of thousands of people to carry the stones needed to rebuild the mighty walls. It is not known what chief first built Kīholo fishpond, but archaeological evidence indicates this man-made fishpond probably existed for hundreds of years before Kamehameha's time.

During his circuit of the island of Hawai'i in 1823, English missionary William Ellis visited Kīholo and noted:

> This village exhibits another monument of the genius of Tamehameha. A small bay, perhaps half a mile across, runs inland a considerable distance. From one side to the other of this bay, Tamehameha built a strong stone wall, six feet high in some places, and twenty feet wide, by which he had an excellent fish pond, not less than two miles in circumference. There were several arches in the wall, which were guarded by stakes driven into the ground so far apart so as to admit water of the sea; yet sufficently close to prevent the fish from escaping. It was well stocked with fish, and water-fowl were seen swimming on its surface.

The flow of 1859 basically destroyed Kīholo. Salt pans carved into the flat *pāhoehoe* lava, remnants of trails, and fallen stone walls remain to offer mute testimony of a once active Hawaiian community. After the eruptions, optimistic builders returned to Kīholo to erect a church, school house and small store to serve the fishermen and their families who still called Kīholo home.

In the early 20th century, Kīholo became the port for Pu'uwa'awa'a Ranch, some ten miles inland near Pu'uanahulu. Cattle were shipped from Kīholo to Honolulu on a regular basis until 1958. The construction of Queen Ka'ahumanu Highway in 1975 ended Kīholo's former isolation and opened the door to residential development there. (7/308)

2. Pu'uanahulu

The small community of Pu'uanahulu is located at Kona's northern edge near the furrowed cinder cone called Pu'uwa'awa'a. (Some Kona residents refer to it as Plum Pudding, Pumpkin, Cupcake or Jello-mold Hill because of its distinctive shape.) Pu'uanahulu sprang to life in the 1890s when the Hawaiian government provided homestead lands in the area to small farmers and ranchers. Among those who took advantage of this opportunity were Eben Parker Low and Robert Hind who started raising sheep and cattle at what would become Pu'uwa'awa'a Ranch. Until then, the region had been sparsely populated by Hawaiian families raising dryland crops.

Pu'uwa'awa'a Ranch included pastures and lava fields that stretched from Hualālai's forested slopes to Kīholo Bay. Ranching in this terrain challenged the ingenuity and endurance of both man and beast. Building fences and stone walls over the jagged lava was a back-breaking job, and, with earthquakes, destructive wild pigs and goats, frequent repairs were necessary. Collecting enough rain water in tanks and reservoirs to keep horses and cattle alive was a constant worry. Branding herds of thousands of cattle required the help of many hands. Two-day cattle drives to Kīholo Bay with half-wild longhorn cattle kept men and horses on their toes. No wonder the people of Puʻuanahulu were known to be expert horsemen and skilled ropers.

Puʻuanahulu's quaint cluster of small homes is a reminder of the days when ranching was the backbone of Kona's agricultural economy. The little Protestant church was built in 1918 by the Reverend Albert S. Baker (section 25) to serve the growing number of residents. For many years the town had its own elementary school which closed in 1964.

For many reasons, ranching at Puʻuwaʻawaʻa Ranch is no longer economically feasible. Puʻuanahulu's dramatic bluff has been sub-divided for private residences and a new golf course, which has changed the rural atmosphere. (1/68)

3. 1801 Lava Flow

The unique and dramatic lava landscape that stretches north from Kona International Airport to Kīholo Bay is dominated by a series of lava flows, the most recent being produced by Hualālai in 1801. Visitors can park at the scenic overlook near Kīholo Bay on Queen Kaʻahumanu Highway (82 mile marker) for a good look at the Kaʻūpūlehu flow's pathway. Another fine viewing spot is on the Hawaiʻi Belt Road (Hwy. 190) near the 27 mile marker, closer to the upper vent from which the Huʻehuʻe flow emerged and poured into the sea at Keahole Point. These two eruptions are commonly called the 1801 lava flow.

Hualalai, owing to the vegetation sparsely sprinkled over it, looks as if it had been quiet for ages, but it has only slept since 1801, when there was a tremendous eruption from it, which flooded several villages, destroyed many plantations and fishponds, filled up a deep bay 20 miles in extent, and formed the present coast. The terrified inhabitants threw living hogs into the stream, and tried to propitiate the anger of the gods by more costly offerings, but without effect, till King Kamehameha, attended by a large retinue of chiefs and priests, cut off some of his hair, which was considered sacred, and threw it into the torrent, which in two days ceased to run. This circumstance gave him greatly increased ascendancy, from his supposed influence with the deities of the volcanoes.

This vivid description was written by author Isabella Bird in 1873 during her famous six-months' sojourn in the Sandwich Islands. The chief "deity of the volcano" not named by Bird was the volcano goddess Pele, who, according to Hawaiian tradition, could appear as fire, a wrinkled hag, a child, or a beautiful girl.

Legend says that Pele was hungry for the fish in Paʻaiea, Kamehameha's largest fishpond on the North Kona coast. When her request for some fish was denied—the unwitting overseer did not realize the old woman in front of him was a goddess—she destroyed the entire coastline in a rage.

Until recently, much of the land covered by the 1801 flow remained barren. Until the completion of Kona International Airport at Keāhole in 1970 and Queen Kaʻahumanu Highway in 1975, access to the coast was impossible except by boat, on horseback, on foot and later by 4-wheel drive vehicle.

Visitors should remember that the 1801 flow is evidence that volcanic eruptions, unpredictable and destructive, are an inescapable part of life for Kona's people. Volcanologists warn that Hualālai is still an active volcano with fireworks long overdue! (3/284; 15/396)

4. Kaʻūpūlehu

Nothing remains at Kaʻūpūlehu to recall the capture of the *Fair American* by Chief Kameʻeiamoku in 1790. However, this historically significant encounter did occur off the North Kona coast, and its outcome directly aided King Kamehameha's quest for power.

Captain James Cook's arrival in the Sandwich Islands in 1778 brought foreign sea captains to Hawaiʻi on a regular basis for the first time in recorded history. Traders, some carrying furs from the Pacific Northwest to China, stopped briefly in Hawaiʻi to procure water, firewood, meat, salt, fruits, and vegetables. Hawaiian chiefs, who controlled all barter with outsiders, wanted western goods such as iron, gunpowder, and firearms in exchange. Most meetings were peaceful. However, the combination of some unscrupulous traders and a few devious chiefs occasionally led to skirmishes, some proving fatal.

In 1789, the American merchant snow *Eleanora* sailed into Hawaiian waters under the command of Simon Metcalfe, a hot-tempered and violent man. On his way to China from Northwest America, Metcalfe planned to meet his son Thomas, captain of the small schooner *Fair American*, during his winter stopover in Hawai'i. As Simon Metcalfe sailed down the west coast of Hawai'i, he antagonized numerous chiefs with his imperious manner. One chief in particular, Kame'eiamoku, insulted and struck by Metcalfe, swore to take revenge on the next foreign ship that appeared.

While Simon Metcalfe waited for his son's arrival in the safety of Kealakekua Bay, the unsuspecting *Fair American* appeared off North Kona's coast enroute to the long-awaited father and son reunion.

Off Ka'ūpūlehu, Kame'eiamoku saw his chance for revenge. The chief and his men attacked the *Fair American*, threw her six crewmen overboard, and beat five of them, including Thomas Metcalfe, to death with canoe paddles. The only survivor was Welshman Isaac Davis. Chief Alapa'i, a brother of Kame'eiamoku, hauled him half-dead into a canoe and took him ashore.

Alerted that a foreign ship had been captured, Kamehameha I put a *kapu* (taboo or prohibition) on Kealakekua Bay. This *kapu* effectively cut off all contact with local Hawaiians or visiting traders for Simon Metcalfe. He never heard the unhappy news of the *Fair American*. While Metcalfe waited for his son's arrival, John Young, an English boatswain from *Eleanora*, went ashore on an excursion. Kamehameha detained him. Metcalfe fired guns repeatedly to guide Young back to the ship, but to no avail. After two days, Metcalfe sailed away without ever learning the fate of his boatswain or his son. Kamehameha immediately went to Ka'ūpūlehu to claim the *Fair American* and Davis.

John Young and Isaac Davis became captains of Kamehameha I's fleet of foreign-built ships, which included the *Fair American*. In time, they married Hawaiian *ali'i* (nobility) and achieved wealth and high status in the Hawaiian Kingdom. Many of their descendents have played prominent roles in Hawaiian history, including Young's granddaughter, Queen Emma, wife of Kamehameha IV.

5. Kaloko-Honokōhau National Historical Park

This 1160-acre shoreline and ocean park encompasses a wealth of ancient Hawaiian archaeological and cultural features, among them ʻAimakapā and Kaloko Fishponds, ʻAiʻopio fish trap, Puʻuoina Heiau, several *kūʻula* (fishing shrines), remains of a *hōlua* (ancient sled course), and numerous petroglyphs. This relatively new park (1978) is still in the early stages of development as a National Park. However, adventuresome visitors will find Honokōhau Beach, tidal pools, natural wetlands, and a scenic coastline an exciting setting in which to learn about early Hawaiian history.

Although Kaloko-Honōkohau may seem arid and inhospitable today, this area once supported a thriving Hawaiian settlement dating back to the 12th century. Within the sheltered waters of man-made fishponds along the seashore, residents raised tasty fish to feed the royal family and its many dependents. Skilled Hawaiians maintained the water quality of the ponds, protected desired species of fish, and chose the proper time to harvest them. The *aliʻi* could demand his favorite *ʻanae* (mullet) or *awa* (milkfish) for dinner any time of year,

Kaloko Fishpond, precontact, ca. 1970. Photograph by Norman Carlson. (Courtesy KHS Archives)

regardless of bad weather, warfare, or famine. According to oral accounts, the fish were delivered so quickly by swift runners to the king's court they would arrive still fresh and wriggling.

Throughout the early 20th century, Hawaiian families lived along this coastline, continuing the traditions of fishing and salt making historically connected to the land. At Christmas and New Year's, Kailua residents would gather before dawn at Akona Store, waiting for the donkeys from Kaloko to arrive. Each donkey carried a bulging pack filled with fresh *awa*. The donkeys knew the trail so well, they could make the trip to Kailua by themselves, while the fishermen hauled in the last of the catch. Kaloko fishpond was still in operation until 1961.

Visitors will find no amenities except restrooms at Kaloko Pond at this time. Visitor information is available at park headquarters located in the Kaloko Light Industrial Park on Kanalani Street. Office hours are Monday through Friday, 7:30 a.m. to 4 p.m., telephone (808) 329–6881. The access gate to Kaloko Pond is open from 8 a.m. to 3:30 p.m. daily, or visitors can park at Honokōhau Harbor and hike north into the park along a coastal trail. (1/21)

6. M. Onizuka Store

Founded in 1933 by Masamitsu Onizuka and his wife Mitsue Nagata, M. Onizuka Store served the people of Keopū, North Kona, for 57 years. As a general merchandise store, it was a convenient one-stop shop filled with tubs of shoyu, tins of Saloon Pilot crackers, 100-pound bags of rice, sacks of salted codfish, and jars of candy. Mr. Onizuka also had a chauffeur's license and ran a taxi service from the store. He was particularly busy on election day driving voters to and from the polling places in Kailua. After her husband passed away, Mrs. Onizuka ran the store until the day of her death in 1990 at the age of 76. Today it is a private residence.

Onizuka Store holds a special place in the hearts of Kona's residents for it was here that Ellison Onizuka, America's first astronaut of Japanese-American descent, and Hawai'i's first astronaut, was raised. His example of a Japanese-American country boy reaching a position of fame and honor throughout the United States made all Hawai'i proud. When he died in the *Challenger* explosion on January 28, 1986, shock and grief at his tragic death was felt worldwide. Onizuka's memory is cherished, especially here in Kona, where friends

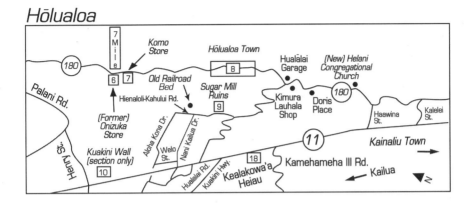

Hōlualoa

and neighbors still remember little Ellison with stars in his eyes playing under the coffee trees.

Although Onizuka Store is not open to the public, visitors may tour the Onizuka Space Center at Kona International Airport for more information about Ellison Onizuka.

Ellison Onizuka, 24 August 1964. Photograph by Adrian Saxe. (Courtesy KHS Archives)

7. K. Komo Store

K. Komo Store has been a welcome oasis for thirsty travelers (and automobiles) since the early 1900s. One of the oldest operating general merchandise stores and gas stations in North Kona, Komo Store's cheerful green and white exterior is typical of a style of architecture popular in the early 1900s in Kona.

Kakuro Komo came to Hawai'i from Hiroshima-ken, Japan, near the end of the 19th century. He worked for Kona Development Company as a locomotive engineer during the days when sugar was big business in *mauka* Kona. Later, he worked for Pu'uwa'awa'a Ranch as a truck driver. His wife, Yoshi Mimaki, came from Yamaguchi-ken as a "picture bride." The Komos settled down in the *ahupua'a* of Keopū to raise a family and work at Kakuro's uncle's store. Ken Komo, Kakuro's youngest son and store owner today, was born at the store in 1928.

Three generations of the Komo family have worked to keep Komo Store a successful enterprise along the *mauka* road. Today, Ken Komo and his wife, Mutsumi, continue the family tradition of serving the nearby community. Although payment is no longer made with bags of coffee, the people of Keopū still grow Kona's famous crop. In fact, the Komos sell their own estate-grown coffee under the KK label at their store.

Hōlualoa Town, Japanese celebration, ca. 1920 (Courtesy KHS Archives)

8. Hōlualoa Town

The lands of Hōlualoa are part of the historic Kona Field System (section 29). Full-scale immigration of Chinese, Portuguese, and Japanese laborers in the 19th century changed Hōlualoa from a Hawaiian farmland to the principal agricultural village in North Kona. Newcomers found the steep countryside suitable for growing coffee, cotton, Isabella grapes, breadfruit, and Kona oranges.

Then, believe it or not, Hōlualoa was a sugar town for 27 years! From 1899 to 1926, coffee was cut down to make way for fields of sugar cane which surrounded Hōlualoa in all directions. The sugar plantation carried the region's economy and Hōlualoa became its commercial center. Plantation camps sprang up near the mill and along the length of the railway (section 9). Catholic, Protestant and Buddhist churches were established to serve the multi-ethnic community.

Clearly, immigrants found Hōlualoa to be a town of financial opportunity. Luther Aungst chose Hōlualoa as headquarters for the Kona Telephone Company started in the 1890s. Using mules to drag telephone poles across lava flows, Aungst installed a line from Hilo to Kaʻū, and across Kona to North Kohala. Dr. Harvey Saburo Hayashi from Aomori-Ken, Japan, one of Kona's first full-time resident physicians and publisher of Kona's first newspaper, the *Kona Echo*, lived there.

Today, long-time residents like Goro Inaba, proprietor of the Kona Hotel, insist that Hōlualoa was a busier spot than Kailua during the first decades of the 20th century. Where the Imin Center is today was the Hōlualoa Japanese language school, the first independent language school in all Hawaiʻi. It was built and maintained by the community and not associated with any religious group. Kona Bottling Works (1920–1942), formerly situated downstairs where the Country Frame Shop is today, supplied and delivered soda water as far south as Hoʻōpūloa.

Sugar's collapse spelled economic ruin for many people. Coffee kept Hōlualoa alive, but just barely. Young people looking for employment left North Kona in droves, finding work in Honolulu or the mainland. By 1958, just over 1,000 people lived in the Hōlualoa area. The construction of Kuakini Highway in the early 1950s reduced traffic through town even further.

Tourism and a coffee boom have brought new life to Hōlualoa Eager entrepreneurs have transformed old garages and empty houses into galleries showcasing art of every description, some of it produced by artists who grew up in Hōlualoa. Friendly family-run businesses such as Kimura's Lauhala Shop, the Kona Hotel, and the thrice-named Paul's Place (formerly Tanimoto General Store in the 1890s, and later Morikami Store in the late 1920s), keep old Kona alive. (10/71–73)

9. 1901 Sugar Mill and Railroad

Commercially grown sugar has totally disappeared from Kona's landscape, but it was big business in the early 20th century. A railroad once ran 11 miles to haul cane from fields in upland Kona as far south as Onouli to the mill above Kailua. In those booming sugar days, cane was planted on any available land above the railroad, leaving only pockets of rocky soil for coffee.

The Kona Sugar Company started in 1899 with ambitious plans to create a major sugar plantation in Kona. The company built Kona's first sugar mill above Kailua village in 1901. In a district famous for its lack of fresh water, the mill site near Wai‘aha Stream at an elevation of 764 feet was considered a likely location. Although the company built a reservoir, there never was enough water to properly process the cane. In 1903, the company went broke.

Other investors later purchased the company, renamed it the Kona Development Company. In 1916, the plantation was bought by a group of Japanese with capital from Tokyo and continued to produce sugar for ten more years. Many Kona youngsters grew up in sugar camps complete with stables, plantation stores, and communal baths for the Japanese laborers. When the plantation collapsed in 1926, that spelled the end of the railroad and Kona's brief stint as a plantation community.

During World War II, the United States Army set up a training camp at the mill site. Once again, the availability of water was of primary importance. Concerned that the mill's tall smokestack would act as a "marker" to attract enemy attention, the Army took the smokestack down, salvaging the metal for scrap iron. From 1942 to approximately 1944, at least three Army regiments passed through this camp to be acclimatized and trained for battle in the Pacific arena.

Kona Development Company, ca. 1920. Photograph by Toyoki Ueda. Note mill's smokestack. (Courtesy Edwin Ueda Collection)

The ruins of the sugar mill can be clearly seen from Hienaloli Road off Hualālai Road. Be sure to notice the large stone embankments built all by hand for the railroad bed. Once planned to run 30 miles through Kona, the West Hawaii Railway Co. was an ambitious project thwarted by Kona's terrain and slow economy. Portions of the old railway bed can be seen at the top of Nani Kailua and Aloha Kona subdivisions; a fine, flat surface for jogging and walking the dog. (10/90–92)

10. Great Wall of Kuakini

The Great Wall of Kuakini is a stone barricade, over 5 miles long, that stretches from Kailua to beyond Keauhou less than a mile from the seacoast. When John Papa I'i recorded his first impressions of Kailua in 1812, he wrote, "A stone wall to protect the food plots stretched back of the village from one end to the other and beyond." It is possible this wall was enlarged during Governor John Adams Kuakini's time to control the increasingly problematic movement of cattle.

Before Polynesians settled these islands, Hawai'i's specialized environment included only two mammal species, the Hawaiian hoary bat and the monk seal. The colonizing Polynesians brought to Hawai'i dogs, pigs, fowl, and the Polynesian rat. These imported animals had an impact on the natural environment, but not as devastating an impact as the animals introduced by European sea captains after Captain James Cook's "discovery."

Cattle, sheep, goats, and large European boars were purposefully brought to the Sandwich Islands to stock western ships with food supplies during their long sea voyages. Captain George Vancouver, determined to establish cattle in Hawai'i, carried seasick bulls and cows across the Pacific Ocean on board his ship two years in a row. In 1794, as special gifts for Kamehameha I, he successfully landed his final shipment of a young bull, two cows and two bull calves at Kealakekua Bay.

The cattle soon adapted to Hawai'i, and, without a single natural enemy, proceeded to trample the countryside. They chewed crops, tender trees, and the sides of thatched houses. They devastated not only gardens, but also the native landscape. Wild bulls chased little children and terrified unwary travelers.

With no knowledge of cattle raising, the Hawaiians were helpless to control the huge animals. Governor Kuakini may have ordered the expansion of the older wall, originally built to stop pigs and dogs from damaging the upland gardens, to put a stop to midnight cattle stampedes through Kailua.

In the 1830s, King Kamehameha III brought Mexican-Spanish cowboys, called Los Espanoles or vaqueros, to Hawai'i to teach his subjects horseback riding, cattle roping, saddle making, and lariat braiding. The Hawaiians learned quickly. Before long, the Hawaiian cowboy, or *paniolo* (named after his Mexican counterpart), became a colorful part of Hawai'i's changing 19th-century culture.

Modern road construction and housing projects have breached Kuakini's Wall in several places. A section remains near the southern edge of Crossroads Center on the *mauka* side of Queen Ka'ahumanu Highway. (10/75, 79; 8/111)

11. Kailua Town

The town of Kailua, which means in Hawaiian two seas or two currents, takes its name from the little inlet just north of Hulihe'e Palace. This small beach is a fragment of a series of much larger white sand beaches which once lined the entire bay, making this area a favorite fishing, surfing, swimming, and boating spot for early Hawaiians. That white sand still exists under the asphalt pavement and concrete seawall first built in 1900 and subsequently rebuilt after World War II.

Once a small Hawaiian village, Kailua grew to become the political, social, and commercial hub of Kona in the 19th century. When Kamehameha I chose Kailua to be his final home, Kailua became the capital of Hawai'i for many years. Historic structures such as Hulihe'e Palace, Moku'aikaua Church, and St. Michael's Catholic Church indicate Kailua's importance as a favorite royal residence and center for early missionary activity.

As one of Kona's few safe natural harbors, Kailua was frequently visited by exploring sea captains, traders, and whalers. Once regular inter-island travel and commerce became established, sailing ships, and later steamers, used Kailua as a regular port-of-call until the mid-1900s.

Boat day was a major bi-weekly event in Kailua for well over a century. Strong Hawaiian sailors would row passengers, cargo, and mail bags ashore, regardless of wind and waves. On the return trip to

Steamer Day, Kamakahonu at Kailua Bay, ca. 1890. Note Moku'aikaua Church and Hulihe'e Palace in the background. (Courtesy Bishop Museum Archives)

Kailua to Keauhou • Map 1

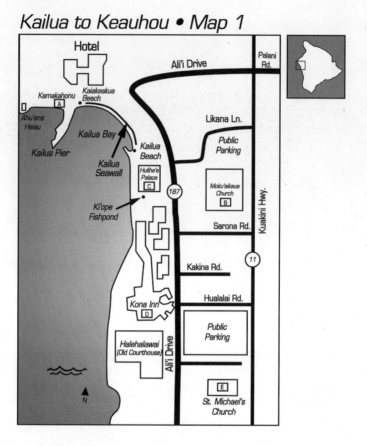

Honolulu, the decks would be crammed with an assortment of ever changing cargo: bags of coffee, stacks of goat and cattle hides, bales of wool, kegs of butter from the mountain dairies, and crates of famous Kona oranges. When sugar was booming in Kona, the smell of molasses and raw sugar wafted across the waters. Passengers, often draped with flower *lei*, traveled with their luggage of *poi* bowls, riding saddles, live chickens, dogs, pigs, and bananas. Bustling stores, small restaurants, boarding houses, *poi* factories, and saloons crowded the shoreline to take advantage of this regular business.

From about 1880 to 1956, local ranchers used Kailua Bay to ship cattle to market in Honolulu. In those noisy and dusty days of the 1800s, the bellowing bullocks were lassoed individually and pulled into the surf by cowboys riding special shipping horses. Spectators loved to watch the cowboys race across the sand of Kaiakeakua Beach

Cattle shipping, Kailua Bay, Kaiakeakua Beach, ca. 1935.
(Courtesy KHS Archives)

(the small beach south of Kailua pier), plunge into the blue Pacific, and then swim on horseback out to waiting whaleboats. The cattle, protesting all the way, were lashed to the gunwales, rowed out to deeper water and then hoisted aboard inter-island steamers. In the 20th century, motorized whaleboats called launches towed the boats loaded with cattle or cargo out to the steamer.

In Kailua's final years as a cattle-shipping town, tug and barge had replaced the colorful steamers to transport livestock and cargo between Honolulu and the neighbor island ports. At Kailua, this type of vessel could tie up to the pier and cattle could walk directly aboard, thanks to a complex of holding pens and cattle chutes built on a new pier. The need to lighter cargo out to a ship was eliminated.

The last shipments by barge left Kailua in 1956 as better roads, bigger cattle trucks, and a new deep water harbor at Kawaihae spelled the end of "Shipping Day" for this Kona town. (16/69; 10/81)

11A. Kamakahonu

Kamehameha I rose to power in Kona in the 1780s as an unbeatable warrior chief and successfully fought to unite the Hawaiian Islands into a single kingdom under his rule. After a lifetime of battles waged across the island chain, the aging ruler returned to the island of his birth with his court in 1812. He chose to live at Kamakahonu (the eye of the turtle), an area named for a distinctive lava formation which has now been covered by the pier. From this small white sand beach, Kamehameha ruled all Hawai'i.

Kamakahonu was once enclosed by a massive crescent shaped stone wall which extended from the site of the modern pier northward to the shoreline beyond the replica of 'Ahu'ena Heiau. Within this four acre enclosure, Kamehameha lived with members of his family, royal attendants, priests, and advisors. He built several thatched dwelling houses, a stone storehouse to hold, among other things, kegs of gunpowder and rum, and rebuilt 'Ahu'ena Heiau.

Kamehameha lived at Kamakahonu for seven years and died there in 1819. He left as principal heir his twenty-two-year-old son Liholiho, called Kamehameha II after his father's death. In a break with previous Hawaiian tradition, Kamehameha I's favorite wife, Ka'ahumanu, claimed her husband's dying wish was that she would rule as *kuhina nui* or regent.

Within months of his father's death, Liholiho defied tradition. The custom in old Hawai'i was for men and women to eat apart, in

'Ahu'ena Heiau, ca. 1819. Lithograph by Louis Choris. Note *kapu* sticks. (Courtesy Bishop Museum Archives)

separate buildings. The punishment for breaking this kapu was death. However, Liholiho chose to eat in public with his mother, Keōpūolani, and Kaʻahumanu at a feast held at Kamakahonu.

This single event, called the *ʻai noa* or "free eating", essentially destroyed the basis of Hawaiʻi's structured society. The ensuing social upheaval tore Hawaiʻi's culture apart, toppling ancient gods and customs almost overnight. It finally took a battle (section 17B) to secure Kamehameha II's survival as king.

In 1820, Liholiho moved his court from Kailua to Honolulu to keep an eye on the activities of whalers, traders, and newly arriving missionaries. He left John Adams Kuakini in charge of the island of Hawaiʻi as governor. Kuakini lived at Kamakahonu until he moved into Huliheʻe Palace in 1838. A large fort erected at Kamakahonu became a prominant feature. Visiting Europeans remarked at the size of its massive walls, 20 feet high and 14 feet thick, topped with a battery of eighteen thirty-two-pound guns.

In 1855, Princess Ruth (*Luka*) Keʻelikōlani became Governess of Hawaiʻi and moved the seat of office from Kailua to Hilo. Kamakahonu crumbled into ruin. King Kalākaua later converted Kamehameha's old stone warehouse into a storage shed for whaleboats. In 1898, Kamakahonu became the Kona headquarters for H. Hackfeld & Co., a German commercial trading company. (The company changed its name to American Factors during World War I after it was purchased by Americans.) In 1959, Amfac transformed its Kailua real estate holdings at Kamakahonu, probably the most historic site in all Kona, into the original King Kamehameha Hotel, Kailua's first high rise hotel.

A lack of appreciation for many of Kona's historic sites has resulted in their loss and destruction. Fortunately, a scaled down replica of ʻAhuʻena Heiau has been built on the site, offering a glimpse of Kamehameha I's world. (1/21; 8/110; 2/33, 47; 5/55)

11B. Mokuʻaikaua Church

This stone and mortar building, completed in 1837, is the oldest surviving Christian church in the state of Hawaiʻi. Built of stones taken from a nearby Hawaiian *heiau* and lime made of burned coral, it represents the new western architecture of early 19th-century Hawaiʻi.

Moku'aikaua Church

Moku'aikaua takes its name from a forest area above Kailua from which timbers were cut and dragged by hand to construct the ceiling and interior.

Christian worship has taken place near this site since 1820, the year the first American Protestant missionaries sailed into Kailua Bay. With the permission of Liholiho (Kamehameha II), the missionaries built a grass house for worship in 1823 and, later, a large thatched meeting house. With the help of Governor Kuakini, missionary Asa Thurston directed the construction of the present Moku'aikaua Church, then the largest building in Kailua. Its massive size indicates the large Hawaiian population living in or near Kailua at that time.

Moku'aikaua, with its 112-foot-tall steeple, is a picturesque reminder of the enthusiasm and energy of the first American missionaries and their Hawaiian converts. Unfortunately, Thurston's large and healthy congregation decreased considerably in the 19th century. In 1824, he reported a population of not less than 20,000 inhabitants in Kona. By 1832, the number had shrunk to 12,432. The census of 1835 reported barely 11,000. These figures reflect the appalling death rate among the native Hawaiians after the introduction of foreign diseases such as the common cold, flu, measles, venereal disease, and tuberculosis. (10/14, 17)

Moku'aikaua Church, ca. 1890. Church constructed ca. 1837.
(Courtesy Bishop Museum Archives)

11C. Hulihe'e Palace

Hulihe'e Palace is Kona's only existing royal residence and one of three remaining in the state. (The other two are Iolani Palace and Queen Emma's Summer Palace, both on O'ahu.) High Chief Kuakini, governor of the island of Hawai'i, built it to be his home in 1838. Constructed of lava rock and coral lime mortar, Hulihe'e's original exterior looked very similar to neighboring Moku'aikaua Church's exposed stone walls.

After Kuakini's death in 1844, Hulihe'e became a favorite retreat for members of the Hawaiian royal family. However, not all of them enjoyed the new Western style of life. For example, Princess Ruth Ke'elikōlani lived at Hulihe'e Palace, but slept in a traditional *pili* grass house on the palace grounds, preferring the Hawaiian manner. She also refused to speak English. Extensive remodeling by King Kalākaua and Queen Kapi'olani in 1884 transformed the original structure to suit the Victorian tastes of the late 19th century.

During Kalākaua's reign (1874–1891), Hulihe'e was the scene

Hulihe'e Palace with Princess Ruth Ke'eilikōlani's grass house, ca. 1885. Photograph by C. J. Hedemann. (Courtesy Hawaii State Archives)

of lively parties and festive dances, befitting the "Merry Monarch." After the overthrow of the monarchy in 1893 and Kapiʻolani's death in 1899, Huliheʻe fell into disrepair. Its overgrown gardens and Kīʻope Spring became a children's playground. A group of enthusiastic card players used to play poker by the light of kerosene lanterns on the palace's front porch.

In 1920, the Inter-Island Steamship Company considered buying Huliheʻe, tearing it down, and building Kona's first seaside hotel on the royal grounds.

When news of this reached the ears of the Daughters of Hawaiʻi in Honolulu, they rushed to the Territorial Legislature and demanded the rescue of the palace.

Now maintained as a museum by the Daughters of Hawaiʻi, Huliheʻe Palace contains a fine collection of ancient Hawaiian artifacts, as well as ornate furnishings that illustrate the lifestyle of the Hawaiian nobility in the late 19th century. Intricately carved furniture, European crystal chandeliers, and immense fourposter beds fill the rooms. Huliheʻe Palace reveals the Hawaiian nobility's passion for western fashions and is a poignant reminder of Kailua's past as a favorite royal residence. (1/21; 2/40; 6/81)

11D. Kona Inn

The Kona Inn, built in 1928, heralded the start of commercial tourism in Kona. The decision by the Inter-Island Steamship Navigation Company to place a hotel in the shadow of Huliheʻe Palace signaled a new era for the isolated and undeveloped village at Kailua. Credit for Kona Inn's graceful design goes to architect Charles Dickey (1871–1942), responsible for many distinctive and well-known buildings throughout Hawaiʻi.

The Kona Inn was built for a wealthy, leisured class. It had a saltwater swimming pool, tennis courts, cocktail lounge, and an unbeatable sunset view. For local residents with money to spend, the Kona Inn offered the amenities of a country club. It was the place to be on New Year's Eve and throughout the year. Hula dancers, *ukulele* players, and singers with a Hawaiian repertoire were now in demand. During World War II, the Inn's bar was a favorite watering hole for military officers.

Why had Kailua taken so long to become a tourist destination?

A major problem was the lack of fresh water. The Kona Inn took over the Kona Development Co.'s abandoned sugar mill water system and piped water to the hotel and the manager's quarters. There was no regular County water system in Kailua until 1953.

Transportation was also a problem. The first commercial flight from Honolulu to the original Kona Airport just north of town landed in 1949. Before that, travel by steamer was the only choice, and they were built primarily for cargo transport with only basic passenger accommodations.

Hawai'i's roads were also terrible, thanks to miles of lava, deep gulches, and steep volcanic slopes. Despite these difficult conditions, the first guests to the Kona Inn arrived via a 121-mile ride in a touring Packard from Hilo via the Volcano. The next day, they took the 97 mile "short cut" back to Hilo via Waimea and the Hāmākua Coast. What a trip! Packing a spare tire and patch kit was standard procedure.

The Kona Inn stopped housing guests in 1976. Today, a shopping complex built in the 1980s sprawls across former gardens and green lawns. The best place to see the famous red roofs is from Kailua pier. (1/45; 6/33)

11E. St. Michael's Church

Built in 1850, St. Michael's Church is the oldest Roman Catholic church in Kona. Although American missionaries received permission to settle in Hawai'i in 1820, the Catholic Church was not officially allowed to be established until 1839. In that year, Kamehameha III issued his "edict of toleration" which guaranteed religious freedom in the Hawaiian Kingdom. The first recorded Roman Catholic service in Kona was held in 1840 just south of Moku'aikaua Church.

Governor John Adams Kuakini gave the land beneath St. Michael's to the Catholic church in 1841, an indication of royal approval for this "new brand" of Christianity. The congregation originally met in a small grass building which stood where the cemetery is today. The present church was completed in 1850 by Father Joachim Marechal and has been restored twice since then.

In 1940, the resident priest, Father Benno Evers, built the coral grotto in front of the church, over the site of the original well. At a time when environmentalists did not caution otherwise, Father Benno had encouraged members of the congregation to fetch 2,500 coral heads from Kailua Bay to construct this unique structure.

St. Michael's is now run by the Maryknoll Fathers who were given responsibility for all North Kona Catholic churches in 1946. (9/390)

12. Hale Hālāwai O Hōlualoa

Hale Hālāwai O Hōlualoa, often called the Hōlualoa Meeting House, was built in 1855 to serve the growing numbers of Hawaiian Christians who lived along the Kona coast. It was built under the supervision of the Reverend John D. Paris, a hard-working Congregational minister who spent the majority of his working life in Kona, building churches and preaching the gospel. Many church members paddled in canoes to Sunday services, pulling their boats up at the sandy canoe landing nearby.

Although it never had a steeple, the meeting house at Hōlualoa

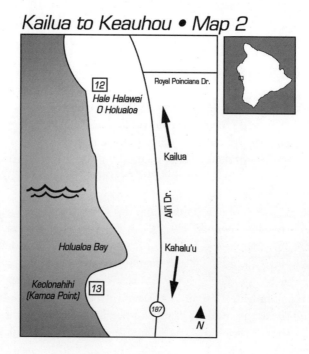

Kailua to Keauhou • Map 2

Kamoa Point, ca. 1890. (Courtesy Helen Weeks Collection)

was used actively as a place of worship throughout the 19th century. The government used it as a school house from 1880 to 1888, and church services continued to be held there until 1920. Later, as many Hawaiian people left their coastal homes to live inland, several old churches were left to crumble. The Hōlualoa Meeting House nearly disappeared entirely.

However, in the 1970s, a congregation of young Christians decided to bring the ruin back to life. Eventually, the new congregation was allowed to worship in the remains of the old stone church which is now listed on the State Register of Historic Places.

From the grassy lawn in front of the church, visitors have a good view of Kamoa Point to the south. Historically a favorite surfing spot, young surfers still find Hōlualoa Bay a great place to ride the waves.

13. Keolonāhihi (Kamoa Point)

Keolonāhihi, located at Kamoa Point, was once perhaps the most significant religious and political site in Kona. At this complex of *heiau*, houses, shrines, and walled enclosures, royal births may have been celebrated; warriors trained in the arts of combat; chiefs taught their genealogies; and priests instructed in their duties. Kamehameha I is said to have learned the skills of warfare and the pleasures of surfing at this place. Later, as a victorious chief, he placed the feathered image of his war god, Kūka'ilimoku, within the sacred temple walls.

When Liholiho overturned the traditional Hawaiian religion in 1819, Keolonāhihi lost its previous significance. As years passed, the stone walls and paved platforms disappeared beneath a tangle of trees and shrubs. Once covering an area of at least 9 acres, the complex has been sliced in half by modern road construction.

In the 1970s, plans to develop Kamoa Point for resort use met strong public resistance as interest in the historic site grew. The State of Hawai'i purchased the Keolonāhihi complex and plans for restoration are underway.

Further investigation has revealed yet another complex of *heiau* and stone enclosures located near Keolonāhihi. This complex was the residence of a high Kona chiefess named Keakealaniwahine and is believed to have been built around 1650 A.D. The Keakealaniwahine complex, however, is located on private land and is possibly being threatened by the construction of a new highway. (8/6, 137, 159)

14. St. Peter's Church and Ku'emanu Heiau

Built in 1880, St. Peter's Church has survived over 100 years thanks to its small size and the devotion of its congregation. It originally stood about one mile north of its present site on a parcel of land near La'aloa Beach, commonly known as Magic Sands Beach.

In 1912, the church was dismantled and carried piece by piece to its present site at Kahalu'u. Donkeys and strong members of the congregation did the heavy work. In 1938, Father Benno, of St. Michael's, added the porch and belfry to the original structure. Since then, St. Peter's has been pushed off its foundation by two separate tsunami (seismic waves). St. Peter's congregation and friends have worked quickly to place the church back where it belongs.

The church sits upon what is said to be the former residence of the *kahuna* (priest) of Ku'emanu Heiau. This stone temple was dedicated to the sport of surfing. Here Hawaiians of old could pray for good surfing weather and, consequently, good sport. Just north of St. Peter's is the main platform or terrace of the *heiau* where chiefs and their families could enjoy watching surfers at Kahalu'u Bay. Nearby is a small brackish pool known as Waiku'i (Pounding Waters), now stagnant and unused. In old Hawai'i, Waiku'i was a place used by chiefs to rinse the salt off after surfing. As the old customs disappeared, the pond became a convenient place to wash clothes in the 19th and early 20th centuries.

Ku'emanu Heiau is part of the Kahalu'u Historic District. (16/120; 18/70)

Kailua to Keauhou • Map 3

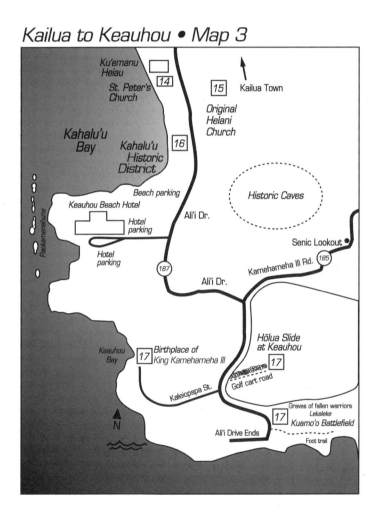

15. Helani Church

The ruins of Helani Church can be seen on the *mauka* side of Aliʻi Drive, just south of St. Peter's Church. This lava rock and coral lime mortar church was built by Rev. John D. Paris in 1861.

After the Hawaiian congregation moved inland and it fell into decay, a new wooden Helani church was erected in 1908 in Kahaluʻu *mauka* along Mamalahoa Highway.

The *heiau* of ʻOhiʻa-Mukumuku (no longer existing) is said to have stood where Helani's ruins are today. Traditionally believed to have been built by the gods, this *heiau* was rededicated by High Chief Lonoikamakahiki to gain strength to defeat the invading Maui chief, Kamalālāwalu, in the 16th century. After his victory, the proud Hawaiʻi chief sacrificed the unlucky invader at nearby Keʻekū Heiau at Kahaluʻu.

Legend states that the Maui chief brought his two dogs, a black blind one and a white one, to his final battle. After the sacrifice of their master, the dogs lay down outside the temple walls and died. Buried

Helani Church, ca. 1906. Church constructed ca. 1861. Photograph by A. S. Baker. (Courtesy Hawaiian Mission Children's Society)

where they lay, the site is said to be still haunted by their faithful presence.

This site is also part of the Kahaluʻu Historic District. (14/42, 43; 18/70)

16. Kahaluʻu Historic District

The area around Kahaluʻu Beach Park was once the site of a busy Hawaiian agricultural and fishing community which thrived until the early 1800s. Kahaluʻu was a favorite residence for many *aliʻi* families who enjoyed Kona's calm weather and the good swimming and surfing at this location. The remains of many *heiau* indicate the presence of an active priesthood, so necessary to ensure the prosperity and power of the ruling class. A stroll along the shore will reveal stone fishing shrines, *heiau*, and house platforms, some intact and others in ruins.

An obvious feature of Kahaluʻu is the man-made breakwater named Pā o ka Menehune which extends partly into the bay. Legend says this stone wall was built by *Menehune*, the residents of ancient Hawaiʻi who were famous for their overnight feats of architectural engineering. The *kahuna* at Kuʻemanu Heiau, afraid of losing the good surfing there if the wall was completed, imitated a rooster and crowed during the night. Fooled into believing that dawn was near, the

Kahaluʻu Complex, ca. 1960. Photograph by Norman K. Carlson. (Courtesy KHS Archives)

Menehune workers left their project incomplete. Now broken up by storms, the remaining stones still protect the waters of Kahaluʻu and shelter the many colorful reef fish living there.

The best way to see Kahaluʻu is to park at Kahaluʻu Beach Park and hike south along the coast line. The grounds of the Keauhou Beach Hotel have been designed with historic sites featured as points of interest. The hotel offers a free 45 minute "Historical Walk" every Monday (10 a.m.) and Thursday (8 a.m.) for the public. Sites visited include a reconstruction of King Kalākaua's beach house, as well as the historic remains of Poʻo Hawaiʻi Pond, Hāpaialiʻi Heiau, and Kapuanoni Heiau. (1/22)

17. Keauhou Bay Area

17A. Kamehameha III Birthplace

At the head of Keauhou Bay is a stone commemorating the birthplace of Kauikeaouli, later called Kamehameha III. On March 17, 1814, Keōpūolani, the highest ranking wife of Kamehameha I, gave birth to her second son near this place, which at the time was surrounded by a well-populated village.

Kauikeaouli was crowned King Kamehameha III at the age of eleven after his older brother, Lihiliho, died of measles in England. His reign (1825–1854) turned out to be the longest in the history of the Hawaiian Monarchy and spanned years of tumultous social, political, and economic change. Tragically, during his reign, he watched half of his Hawaiian subjects die of foreign diseases.

At the request of his mother, one of the first Hawaiian converts to Christianity, Kauikeaouli began his education at the hands of Protestant missionaries at the age of six. After his mother's death in 1823, he continued his studies and, eventually, as king, inspired a virtual educational revolution in the islands. He signed Hawaiʻi's first written constitution and instituted sweeping changes in the traditional pattern of land ownership in 1848. These new land laws, collectively known as "The Great Mahele" (The Great Division), allowed Hawaiians and non-Hawaiians to purchase Hawaiian lands for the first time. He is also fondly remembered as the originator of what later became the State of Hawaiʻi's motto: "*Ua mau ke ea o ka ʻaina i ka pono* (The life of the land is preserved by righteousness)." (9/263–265, 422; 5/73; 10/36)

17B. Kuamoʻo Battlefield

Before Kamehameha I died, he named two heirs to his kingdom. To his son, Liholiho, he left his lands and political power. To his warrior nephew, Chief Kekuaokalani, he entrusted his feathered war god, Kūkaʻilimoku, a powerful symbol of strength, said to utter cries during battle. After Kamehameha's death, Liholiho, encouraged by powerful queens, initiated "free eating" at Kamakahonu and declared the old gods dead. Naturally, this angered many Hawaiians, among them Kekuaokalani, who wanted no part of this unexpected "revolution."

In December of 1819, just seven months after the death of Kamehameha I, the allies of his two opposing heirs met in battle on the jagged lava fields south of Keauhou Bay. Liholiho had more men, more weapons, and more wealth to ensure his victory. He sent his prime minister, the wily Kalanimoku, to defeat his stubborn cousin.

Kekuaokalani marched up the Kona coast from Kaʻawaloa and met his enemies at Lekeleke, just south of Keauhou. The rebel army fought with rusty muskets, as well as with the spears, slingstones, and clubs of old Hawaiʻi. Kalanimoku fielded a large force of well armed and experienced warriors, accustomed to fighting in close quarters. A swivel gun mounted on a double canoe increased their firepower. In spite of this advantage, the first encounter went in favor of Kekuaokalani. At Lekeleke, the king's army suffered a temporary defeat.

Regrouping his warriors, Kalanimoku fought back and trapped the rebels further south along the shore in the *ahupuaʻa* of Kuamoʻo. There, pinned between two armies, one on land and the other in a flotilla of canoes along the coast, Kekuaokalani met defeat and death. His valiant wife, Manono, fought bravely on, falling dead beside him at the battle's end. They are buried together in a stone grave still standing at Kuamoʻo, not visible from the paved highway.

Liholiho ordered the bodies of his men to be buried beneath the terraced graves at Lekeleke, visible today at the end of Aliʻi Drive.

Kekuaokalani's dead warriors were allowed to be buried as well and Liholiho pardoned all the surviving rebels. It is estimated that hundreds of people were killed in this battle, the last fought in Kona.

The battle of Kuamoʻo effectively crushed any hope of reviving the traditional Hawaiian religion and its accompanying *kapu* system. Not every custom died out overnight, but without the direct support of Liholiho, his chiefs, and his *kāhuna,* the ancient religion of the high *aliʻi* could not survive. However, many Hawaiians continued to honor their personal family gods, their *ʻaumakua.*

Liholiho did not know it, but as he celebrated the destruction of one religion, another was making its way toward the shores of his tiny kingdom. In just a few months, the brig *Thaddeus* would drop anchor in Kailua Bay and American missionaries would bring a new god to Kona's people. (8/140; 5/56; 12/102)

17C. Ka Hōlua O Kāneaka

The Hawaiian nobility loved sports of all kinds including surfing, wrestling, swimming, spear throwing, and bowling. Among the most spectacular of these activities was sledding, not on snowy hills, but on grass-covered slopes and stone ramps called *hōlua.* From Keauhou looking *mauka,* (park along Aliʻi Drive across the street from the Keauhou Country Club) the remains of a mile long *hōlua* are still visible. On this manmade stone ramp, skilled sledders using *papa hōlua* (wooden sleds) swooped from the top of Puʻu o Kaomi down to the shore of Heʻeia Bay below.

Although the lower section of this *hōlua* has been destroyed by earthquakes, cattle, and construction, it was once the longest in all Hawaiʻi. It is believed Kamehameha I built it to honor the birth of his son Kauikeaouli in 1814. The slide was up to 50 feet wide in some places with a surface of hard packed dirt and smooth pebble and stone paving.

Before a race, the slide was covered with stems of *pili* grass or alternately, compressed sugarcane leaves. The hot noonday sun made the grass very slippery, so the contestants had the best chance of riding their wooden sleds all the way to the bottom of the course. Both men and women took part in this royal sport, much to the delight of spectators who often made bets on who the winner might be.

Kealakōwaʻa Heiau

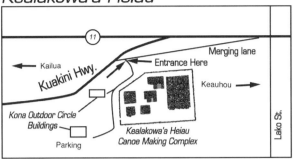

It is estimated that hundreds, if not thousands, of workers were needed to carry the stones, pack the dirt, and collect the grasses needed to construct a complete *hōlua*. Obviously, this type of amusement was only possible for a king or high-ranking chief. After the death of Kamehameha I, few, if any, races took place at Keauhou.

In 1966, this *hōlua* was registered as a National Historic Landmark. Visitors interested in seeing a *papa hōlua* can find a half-size replica at Huliheʻe Palace. (13/224)

18. Kealakōwaʻa Heiau

Kealakōwaʻa (the path of the canoe) is possibly the only surviving canoe-making *heiau* that can be found today in the State of Hawaiʻi. It stands within a complex of several stone walls and platforms that once made up a *kukulu waʻa* (canoe-building compound). This site is positioned on an old Hawaiian trail that once led from Mokuʻaikaua Forest above to Hōlualoa Bay below. Kuakini Highway, surveyed in the mid-1950s, was realigned *mauka* to avoid destroying this unique structure.

The Polynesians were master canoe builders. Wherever they settled across the wide Pacific, they learned how to use local trees and plant fibers to make canoes of sleek design and durability. Migrating Polynesians found a beautiful endemic tree to carve in Hawaiʻi, the mighty *acacia koa*. Once growing luxuriantly across Kona's upper slopes, vast stands of *koa* have been decimated by sheep and cattle during the last two hundred years.

The Kona Outdoor Circle (K.O.C.) now maintains this *heiau* as

Central Kona • Map 1

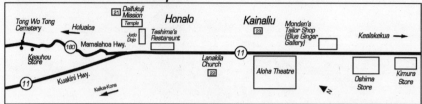

an historic site. Visitors may park in K.O.C.'s parking lot and tour the site at any time. Be aware that finding the entrance to K.O.C. at the junction of Kuakini and Queen Ka'ahumanu Highway can be a tricky maneuver. (13/126)

19. Tong Wo Tong Cemetery

This Chinese cemetery is marked by an ornate archway which reads in English and in Chinese "Tong Wo Tong Cemetery." This gate was built in 1903 by Yoshisuke Sasaki, the builder-owner of Sasaki Store, now named Keauhou Store. The Kona Chinese cemetery is private property and visitors are asked not to tresspass.

Ancestors of Kona's Chinese community are buried in this cemetery. Although it now looks abandoned, in the past, there was a pavillion on the grounds called Bow On Sheh (Protect Peace Club) where families could meet for meals. At annual Ching Ming ceremonies in April, families gathered to "sweep the graves" and make memorial offerings of flowers, food, and incense to departed loved ones. After the pavillion burned, a caretaker's cottage remained on the property until it also burned down years later.

The first Chinese laborers arrived to work on Hawaiian sugar plantations in 1852, although a few Chinese lived in the islands before that date. By the mid-1860s, more Chinese lived in the Hawaiian Islands than Caucasian men.

In Kona, Chinese were among the first successful small storekeepers. Wong Yuen Store, Kim Chong's and Fong Lap's in Kailua, and Lee Hop's in Keauhou *mauka* sold general merchandise, as well as Chinese specialities such as tea cookies and delicious "crack seed." Other Chinese men worked for wealthy immigrant families as cooks or houseboys. Some married Hawaiian women and raised a new generation of Chinese-Hawaiian children to enhance Kona's growing multi-ethnic population.

20. Keauhou Store

Keauhou Store, formerly Sasaki Store, was started in 1919 by Yoshisuke Sasaki. Sasaki was a skilled carpenter from Japan who came to Kona in search of economic opportunity. He earned his first money making coffins out of redwood and then built redwood water tanks for prominent immigrant families.

Recognized as a capable designer, Sasaki built the archway for the Tong Wo Tong Cemetery and helped with the construction of the Daifukuji Soto Mission. After his carpenter's shop in nearby Honalo burned down, he moved to the store site with his wife, Kuma, and their family. Besides building and operating his store, he farmed several acres of coffee. His son, Rikiyo Sasaki, operates the store today.

With its handy gas pump and wide assortment of merchandise, Keauhou Store was a popular place for local coffee farmers and nearby residents to shop. Poor roads and lack of transportation encouraged support of neighborhood stores. With the extension of Highway 11 (Kuakini Highway) in 1967, traffic that formerly passed by Keauhou Store's front porch on Mamalahoa Highway was diverted. Keauhou Store has struggled to survive as discount supermarkets lure customers

Coffee farmer with donkey, 1934. Photograph by UH Agricultural Experiment Station. (Courtesy KHS Archives)

to Kailua, but Rikiyo wants Keauhou Store to remain a part of Kona's *mauka* landscape.

21. Daifukuji Soto Mission

This Buddhist temple was dedicated on May 27, 1921, fulfilling the dream of the Reverend Kaiseki Kodama, founder of the first Kona Soto Mission in 1914. Before its construction, Kodama held services in nearby Hanato Store and other temporary quarters. The present temple was designed and built in part by Yoshisuke Sasaki, the owner of Keauhou Store. Over the years, a social hall, minister's living quarters, and rooms for a Japanese School enlarged the 1921 structure.

In 1926, the Kealakekua Japanese Language School was opened here under Reverend Hosokawa. Mrs. Hosokawa also assisted at the Nāpo'opo'o Japanese Language School several miles south of Honalo. Japanese school at night helped to promote education for women. Although this language school was closed during World War II, it was the first school to be reopened after the war in 1948.

In July of each year a colorful celebration, the O Bon festival, featuring traditional Japanese folk dances and singing, is held at the temple and visitors are welcomed.

22. Lanakila Church

Completed in 1867, Lanakila was the last church built in Kona under the direction of the Reverend John D. Paris. To this day it remains an active Congregational church which proudly maintains its Hawaiian heritage.

Life in 19th-century Kona for Hawaiians was a time of rapid and unrelenting change. The death of Kamehameha I, the collapse of the *kapu* system, the easy availability of firearms and alcohol, the complicated new laws governing land ownership, all these changes created confusion and uncertainty among Kona's rural people. Some Hawaiian residents may have longed for "the good old days." Against this backdrop of subdued frustration, it is not surprising confrontations between newcomers and native Hawaiians sometimes led to violence.

One of Kona's most notorious 19th-century incidents was the

Kaona Uprising. History records that Kaona's discontent may have started here at Lanakila Church.

In Rev. Paris's own words:

> In the year 1867 Mr. Kaona introduced himself to me, saying that he was from Kainaliu, North Kona, and that he had now come back to reside and make Kona his home. He added, 'I have brought with me a lot of Hawaiian Bibles for gratuitous distribution, and I want a place to store them until after the Sabbath.' This was on Saturday afternoon. He begged permission to store them in the new Lanakila church, which was not yet completed. The church lunas voted him permission, and he accordingly stored the Bibles in the unfinished structure.

Not content with storing the Bibles in the church, Kaona and his large family soon took over Lanakila as their residence. Understandably upset, Paris forced Kaona's eviction from the church by order of Governess Keʻelikōlani. Determined to remain nearby, Kaona's followers moved a few hundred yards away from the church, pitched their tents, built thatched shanties, and lived for several months on a neighbor's private property.

Hunger and cold rains eventually forced the religious commune to move to the warmer *makai* elevation at Kainaliu Beach. However, Kaona was still trespassing. When Kona's chief local law officer, Sheriff Neville, served Kaona with a notice of eviction, the religious leader refused to budge. According to Paris, "the rebel spat on the paper, tore it into pieces and stamped upon it."

During 1868, a series of terrific earthquakes shook the entire island for months. Kaona convinced his followers, now numbering in the hundreds, the end of the world was at hand. He announced that he, Kaona, was the only true prophet of Jehovah, and that everyone would be destroyed except his faithful band. Sheriff Neville decided during these excitable times to ride into Kaona's camp and serve his final eviction notice, declaring to Paris that this time he was determined to use force, if necessary. A violent encounter ensued, resulting in the bloody death of Sheriff Neville and one native policeman.

As Paris wrote,

> Kaona harangued his followers to fire the houses and kill all the haoles, heretics and enemies of Jehovah. In the evening the foreigners organized and armed themselves to protect the community, the magistrate of South Kona calling for volunteers to protect life and property.

One can imagine the tense night that followed as isolated families wondered if they would be attacked next. Troops arrived shortly from Honolulu on board the steamer *Kilauea* to put down the rebellion and capture the rebels. Kaona was sentenced to 20 years imprisonment for murder in the second degree, but he was later pardoned by King Kalakaua and set free. He died in Kona in 1883.

History reveals that cultures in turmoil will seek inspirational leaders, and such a man was Kaona. How the historian wishes that Kaona had written his own account of the uprising so modern judgment could be based on hearing both sides of the story. (5/188; 14/50–54)

23. Kainaliu Town

Kainaliu still fits a description written of it in 1958 when its estimated population was 362 people with 34 businesses: "Rural village centered on small commercial strip." One of North Kona's principal business areas, many shops have been operated by the same families for generations.

When Lanakila Church was built in 1867 to serve the resident Hawaiians, the town of Kainaliu probably did not exist. It took the growth of sugar, coffee, and ranching to support Kainaliu's commercial

Kainaliu Town, parade, ca. 1920. (Courtesy KHS Archives)

development. By 1920, numerous small stores lined the street to sell fresh produce and dry goods to the predominantly Japanese residents. Many of the stores boasted handy hitching posts to tie up the donkeys who carried home the 100-pound sacks of rice and 50-pound bags of flour.

Landmarks include the Aloha Theatre built in 1932, Oshima Store started in 1926, and H. Kimura Store (with its well known fabric collection) started in 1927. The building now called the Blue Ginger Gallery was once the Monden tailor shop, one of the few buildings to survive the devastating fire of 1946.

24. Kona Hongwanji Mission

In 1897, Buddhists of the Shin sect in Kona built their first temple in Hoʻokena, South Kona. Two years later, the mission was moved to Kainaliu and moved again in 1906 to its present site in central Kona. The original temple at this site was dedicated in 1907. It underwent several major renovations in the years that followed until it was replaced in 1980 by the temple seen today. The stone arch fronting the temple facing Mamalahoa Highway was built in 1915. Another item of interest is the sculpted image of Amida Buddha in the main altar, carved in sandalwood and consecrated in 1933.

The mission has served Kona's Shin Buddhist community over the past century by first meeting the needs of the immigrant *issei* (first generation), then of the *nisei* (second generation), and today of the *sansei* and *yonsei* (third and fourth generations). Important as a spiritual center, it also has provided many social, cultural, educational, and even economic resources for a population which, particularly in the early days, sometimes spoke little or no English.

25. Central Kona Union Church

Built in 1855 by Reverend John D. Paris, Central Kona Church, or Popopiʻia, is a fine example of the lava rock and mortar buildings erected by missionaries throughout Hawaiʻi in the 19th century. This church served a Hawaiian congregation for many years. In the early

Dedication of Kona Hongwanji Buddhist Mission, Central Kona, 1906. Photograph by A. S. Baker. (Courtesy KHS Archives)

20th century, as the Hawaiian population dwindled, the church attracted a multi-ethnic congregation which reflected the new immigrant groups moving to the Kona. The Reverend Albert S. Baker, Central Kona's minister from 1905 to 1919, noted the numbers in his journal, later recorded by his daughter Ruth Loucks in his biography:

> At the start of 1913 Bert noted that the membership of Central Kona Church consisted of fifteen Japanese, twelve Hawaiians, twelve Americans, two Chinese, two Portuguese, one German, eleven Hawaiian-American, ten Hawaiian-Chinese, and one Hawaiian-Portuguese by birth. Bert was delighted with this diversity.

Like Paris before him, Baker arrived in Kona filled with missionary zeal and a builder's skill. Educated at Amherst, Harvard Medical School and Yale Divinity School, Baker soon discovered he was needed not only as a minister, but as a doctor, lawyer and marriage counselor as well. His mother, Ruth Baker, lived with him throughout his ministry and was the first woman licensed to preach by the Hawaiian Board.

Fast growing Kona experienced a wide variety of problems which Baker tried to address through his church work and in civic clubs. Poor roads, lack of public sanitation, animal abuse, wife

Central Kona • Map 2

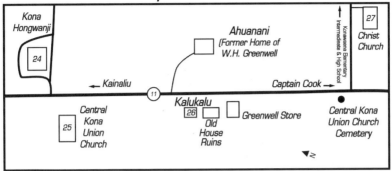

beating, and drunkenness were just a few. He helped organize the Anti-Tuberculosis Society, served as vice president for Hawai'i of the Territory Anti-Saloon League, and spearheaded the formation of the Kona Improvement Club in 1911. One of its first tasks was to fight the Mediterranean fruit fly which was attacking Kona oranges. As chairman of the school committee, he asked for a change in Kona school vacations to permit students to pick coffee during the fall harvest. (This schedule started in 1932.)

Kona had leprosy as well. Baker tried to explain why it was necessary to isolate leprosy patients, but families hid their victims, knowing anyone with leprosy would be sent away to Moloka'i for the rest of their lives. In 1911, seventeen lepers were taken from Kona, but, according to Baker's notes, there were still some left. (12/70, 66, 87, 81)

26. Kalukalu

26A. Kalukalu Homestead

Kalukalu Homestead was the center of Henry Nicholas and Elizabeth Caroline Greenwell's life in Kona for over 80 years. Greenwell, a young Army officer, left England's military life at the age of 23 for adventure in Australia and the California gold fields. Injured while unloading his mining supplies from a ship in San Francisco harbor, he traveled to the Hawaiian Kingdom in 1850 in search of a good physician.

After he recovered, he found Kona's gentle climate perfect for growing oranges, pumpkins, and coffee. He purchased 300 acres of

Kalukalu Homestead—Greenwell family, ca. 1890.
(Courtesy Bishop Museum Archives)

land at Kalukalu in 1850 and began his busy career as farmer, storekeeper, sheep station owner, rancher, postmaster, school agent, and collector for customs at Kealakekua Bay. He married in 1868 and, with the able assistance of his wife, raised ten children at Kalukalu, educating all of them at home.

By the time he died in 1891, Henry Greenwell had witnessed the transformation of Kona's agricultural economy. When he arrived, small Hawaiian family gardens covered the district. By the end of the century, large and small sections of land, owned or leased by immigrants, stretched from the seashore to the high mountain slopes. While some entrepreneurs attempted large-scale sugar, coffee, and cotton plantations, Greenwell utilized Kona's rocky, and sometimes arid lands, to raise sheep for wool, dairy cattle for butter, and, finally, beef cattle to export to Honolulu's butcher shops.

Greenwell's original home at Kalukalu was torn down in the 1960s, but the store he built in approximately 1875 is intact. (10/81)

26B. Greenwell Store

In approximately 1875, H.N. Greenwell built his stone store, establishing Kalukalu as an important commercial outpost in an isolated but growing district. Until this time, stores and warehouses were located along the seashore, at the ports of Kailua, Keauhou, Nāpoʻopoʻo, and Hoʻokena. With the construction of better wagon roads, it was finally possible to haul goods from the coastal docks up to the growing population of *mauka* Kona.

This building served the community as a post office, general merchandise store, and meeting place. Mrs. Greenwell became known throughout Kona as a storekeeper, working with the help of her daughters into her nineties behind the wooden counters. Greenwell family members used the store as a sewing room, ranch office, and warehouse. Morning tea was always served in the store, complete with cream, sugar, and freshly buttered brown bread. The store continued to provide basic supplies and food items for ranch employees until the mid-1950s under the direction of Mrs. Maud Greenwell, widow of William Henry Greenwell, the eldest Greenwell son.

This stone store is the oldest surviving store in Kona and one of the oldest buildings in the district. It is on both the State and the National Register of Historic Places and is remarkable for its lava rock and lime mortar walls. The original roof material was slate which was replaced in the 20th century by corrugated metal roofing. Visitors are sure to notice Greenwell's initials marked on each plank of the ceiling lumber.

26C. D. Uchida Coffee Farm

The D. Uchida Coffee Farm is home to Kona's only living history program dedicated to telling the story of Kona's pioneer Japanese coffee farmers. Homesteaded in 1900 by Japanese immigrants, Daisaku and Shima Uchida took over the farm's lease in 1913. They and members of their family lived and worked at the 6-acre coffee and macadamia nut orchard until 1994.

The structures on this site today were built in 1925 and 1926: a single-wall, board and batten house; redwood tanks for water storage; a small Japanese bath house (*furo*); and a coffee mill typical of Kona's rural coffee lands. The Uchida family left the house in 1994 completely intact.

With the help of the Kona coffee farming community, the Kona Historical Society has undertaken a unique project to preserve, restore and interpret this important resource. Amid pressures to urbanize and modernize Kona, the Uchida Coffee Farm recalls a way of life that is fast disappearing from the Kona landscape. Tours may be arranged through the Kona Historical Society.

27. Christ Church

Christ Church is the oldest Anglican church in the State of Hawai'i. It was built in 1867 by a young English clergyman, the Reverend Charles George Williamson, to serve Kona's tiny but growing Anglo-European community. Sixty Europeans and twenty-five Hawaiians attended the first services.

The Anglican Church was established in Hawai'i in 1862 at the request of King Alexander Liholiho (Kamehameha IV) and his wife, Queen Emma, both of whom were pro-British monarchs. While in Kona, Queen Emma worshipped at Christ Church, filling the church to overflowing with her devoted subjects. Later, King Kalākaua attended Christ Church during his Kona sojourns at Hulihe'e Palace in the 1880s. With the overthrow of the Hawaiian monarchy in 1893 and the annexation of Hawai'i to the United States, Hawai'i's Anglican Church became Episcopalian. (5/158, 159)

28. Captain Cook Coffee Company (Macfarlane Building)

The Macfarlane Building, named after longtime manager Lewis J. Macfarlane, was once the headquarters of Captain Cook Coffee Co. Ltd., one of two companies that controlled over half of the Kona coffee crop during the first half of the 20th century. Restored to serve as a county courthouse in the 1980s, this building is now privately owned.

Captain Cook Coffee Co. Ltd. and H. Hackfeld and Company (later American Factors) acted as the "middle men" or factors between the local farmers and the world coffee market. American Factors advanced farm necessities and foodstuffs through affiliated stores (mostly operated by Japanese merchants) under the condition that farmers were to pay for their merchandise in coffee once the harvest was complete. All this coffee was processed at company mills, American Factor's in Kailua and Captain Cook's at the mill on

Captain Cook Coffee Co. Ltd., Kaʻawaloa, South Kona, ca. 1920.
(Courtesy KHS Archives)

Nāpoʻopoʻo Road (section 33). In this way, two companies dominated the industry with the farmer having no control over the value of his crop.

In the mid-1950s, Captain Cook Coffee Co. and American Factors withdrew from the coffee business. Several coffee cooperatives formed to market Kona's crop, among these being Sunset Co-op which took over operations at the Nāpoʻopoʻo Mill. (10/115–118)

29. Amy B. H. Greenwell Ethnobotanical Garden

The Amy B. H. Greenwell Ethnobotanical Garden is a delight for those visitors interested in Kona's Hawaiian agricultural past. Dozens of native and Polynesian-introduced plants which were used by Hawaiians for food, clothing, lumber, dyes, medicine, canoes, and even a narcotic drink can be found at this unique site owned by the Bishop Museum. Remnants of low stone walls, called *kuaiwi*, mark the boundaries of prehistoric agricultural plots set up by Hawaiians and can still be seen.

Early Hawaiians were master gardeners. With little more than a

South Kona

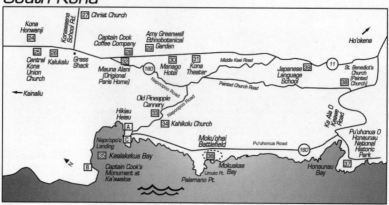

digging stick, called an 'o'o, they cultivated vast amounts of food. In Kona's dry terrain, Hawaiian farmers perfected dry-land methods of mulching, terracing, and planting.

Appreciating the importance of dependable food sources, Kamehameha I built a large garden called Kuahewa on the slopes of Hualālai above Kailua. This garden lay within what historians call the Kona Field System, a vast dry-land farming network 3 miles wide and 18 miles long. It stretched from above Kailua in the north to Kealakekua in the south, including the land in the ethnobotanical garden.

After the arrival of Captain James Cook in 1778 and access to the first metal pick, Hawaiian gardens began to change. Immigrants planted Irish potatoes instead of taro. Imported horses and cattle trampled the fields and knocked down the stone walls. Numerous tropical pests like guava plants, lantana and prickly pear cactus were introduced, unwittingly or on purpose, which spread over the countryside. Where taro and sweet potatoes once grew in tidy plots, shaded by breadfruit, sugarcane, and bananas, imported crops like macadamia nuts and coffee trees, avocados and papayas began to flourish.

This is not true on the grounds of the garden where Amy Greenwell lived until her death in 1974. Although she grew masses of roses and other exotic plants, her first love was Hawai'i—its history, its people, and the amazing culture she knew had once existed so successfully right in her own backyard. An amateur archaeologist who worked along with eminent Bishop Museum staff on the island of Hawai'i, Amy recognized a *kuaiwi* when she saw one. An avid gardener, she also co-authored the fifth volume of *Flora Hawaiiensis* with botanist Otto Degener.

It was Amy Greenwell's dream that her gift to the Bishop Museum would preserve a precious piece of old Hawai'i she saw quickly disappearing. Today, her bequest provides the only public access to the archaeological features of the ancient Kona Field System.

The garden is open to the public from dawn to dusk, seven days a week. Office hours are from 7:00 A.M. to 3:30 P.M., Monday through Friday. For further information and visiting hours call 323-3318. (10/71–74, 4/106, 107)

30. Manago Hotel

Kona's oldest operating hotel began as a two-room house bought with borrowed money in 1917. In the early 1900's, Kinzo Manago came to Hawai'i from Japan planning to work in the sugar fields. Discovering plantation work was not for him, he moved to Kona. He married his picture bride wife, Osame, in 1912, and for four years made a living chopping firewood. With a loan of $100 from his former boss, he bought a tiny house in South Kona, a cookstove, and some supplies in 1917. The Managos probably never dreamed they would one day own a 64-room hotel.

The popularity of the tiny business grew. Osame planted a vegetable garden to keep the restaurant stocked with fresh produce. Additional rooms and a second floor enlarged the original house. Customers asked if they could spend the night, so the Managos provided Japanese futons and rented floor space at $1 a night. By 1929, the Managos had a large family of seven children to feed and clothe, and they were a big help at the ever-enlarging hotel.

Kinzo and Osame's legacy of a family-run hotel continues because their grandchildren manage the business today. Visitors from around the world can enjoy delicious home-cooked meals in the restaurant and examine old photographs hanging in the hotel lobby.

31. Kona Theater

Kona was once filled with movie theatres, large and small, built to entertain residents eager for entertainment and social activity. After all, during the 1920s and 1930s, an era of few cars and no electricity in Kona's rural countryside, going to a movie was pretty darn exciting.

Kona's first theatres, like Goto's Kealakekua Theatre next to Manago Hotel, were simple affairs with dirt floors, no sound systems (movies were silent) or seats. Moviegoers brought their own cushions or tatami mats to sit on. With such a mixed audience—Hawaiian, European, Japanese, Portuguese, Filipino—a wide variety of movies was always in demand. So popular were movies that the community of Hōnaunau built its own theatre.

Kona Theater, an impressive building for Kona at the time, was built in 1929 by Tamajiro Morimoto, an industrious storekeeper who bought and sold coffee to American Factors. (An interesting fact is that his son, Masaji Morimoto, was Hawai'i's first Japanese Territorial Supreme Court Justice.) After years of thrilling Kona residents with samurai films and double features, Kona Theater and Kainaliu's Aloha Theatre, its chief rival, both closed down in the 1970s. Kailua's growing population demanded modern facilities near the tourist centers.

32. Mauna 'Alani (1853 John D. Paris Home)

When the Reverend John D. Paris returned to Hawai'i in 1851, he was assigned to the South Kona mission field. Having lost his first wife to illness while stationed in Ka'u (1841–1847), Paris prudently decided to build his home at a higher, cooler, and, perhaps, healthier elevation. He chose the site of an abandoned missionary health station located at Ka'awaloa *mauka*, overlooking Kealakekua Bay.

He built his stone kitchen and cistern in 1852. The two-story house was completed in 1853. As Paris wrote in his journal, "The lumber for it was sawed in the forest and carried down. The frame is of ohia and the clapboards and shingles of koa." Although the original stone kitchen was ruined in the 1951 earthquake, the house survived.

It is possibly the oldest wooden framed structure standing in *mauka* Kona today.

Paris called his new home Mauna 'Alani, or Orange Hill, after two "very productive" old orange trees he found growing nearby. He believed these trees were some of the original seedlings brought to Kona in 1792 by Archibald Menzies, surgeon and naturalist on board Captain George Vancouver's ship the *Discovery*. According to Paris' great-granddaughter who lives at Mauna 'Alani today, the trees are still bearing.

This private home is not open to the public but can be seen clearly on the *mauka* side of Nāpo'opo'o Road close to the junction with Highway 11. Look for a 2-story white building with a red roof. (14/36; 10/66)

33. Old Pineapple Cannery

A familiar landmark on lower Nāpo'opo'o Road is the old coffee mill, originally built to process pineapple, a crop that never became a commercial success in Kona. The man behind this scheme was W. W. Bruner who came to Kona as a road builder in the 1890s. He later started a pineapple plantation and built his pineapple cannery in 1900 or 1901. When his venture failed, Captain Cook Coffee Company bought the building and converted it to a coffee mill in 1909. Portions of this mill are still in use as part of the Kona Pacific Farmers Cooperative which has processed Kona coffee and macadamia nuts at the mill since 1956.

The Royal Aloha Coffee Mill Museum attached to the old mill is open to the public. Old photographs illustrating the history of Kona coffee and a Japanese bottle collection are on display.

Boom or bust coffee prices have affected coffee farmers in Kona for over 150 years. When coffee prices were high, companies formed large plantations and planted thousands of acres of coffee.

In 1898, just when production was booming, the price of coffee dropped from 27 cents a pound to 15.8 cents. Practically overnight, large plantations collapsed and were broken into small parcels of land. This was an opportunity for Japanese and Portuguese laborers to lease 3 to 5 acre plots, paying rent with a percentage of the coffee crop, typically half the crop.

There were always problems. In the 1850s, white scale blight attacked the coffee orchards and many early plantations failed. In 1905, green scale blight and sooty molds ruined Kona crops. Desperate farmers washed their coffee leaves by hand with soapy water or kerosene emulsion to save the trees. During World War I, coffee could not be shipped to the mainland because of shipping shortages. During the Great Depression, coffee prices plunged and many farmers faced financial ruin.

Kona coffee's ups and downs have had a major impact on this district's history. Fortunately, happy days are here again for coffee farmers in the 1990s. (10/116, 117)

34. Kahikolu Church

Kahikolu Church marked the start of Rev. John D. Paris' church-building career in Kona after his return to the mission field in 1852. As he wrote later:

> The first church which I erected in South Kona was the Kahikolu, or Trinity, Church near Kealakekua Bay. This church is on the site of the immense stone and adoby building erected in 1840 under the supervision of Brethern Forbes and Ives. (The roof of this old church had fallen in and complete rebuilding was found necessary.) The new Kahikolu Church was built of lava rock, taking the width of the old building for the length of the new one. For the lime, coral was cut from the bottom of the ocean by the Hawaiians. I had a hole dug and built a lime kiln where the coral was burned. The lime thus obtained was of good quality and was used for making mortar as well as for finishing the interior of the building. The heavy timbers were dragged from the forest, and the koa shingles and lumber for pulpit and pews were brought from the koa forest a number of miles up the mountainside.

Kahikolu fell victim to time, termites, earthquakes, and the gradual dispersal of its congregation. By the second half of the 20th century, it was a dangerous ruin. A grassroots effort restored the church in 1986 and it once more boasts an active congregation.

Kahikolu is the final resting place of Henry 'Ōpūkahai'a, the famous Hawaiian boy who inspired the first Protestant American missionaries to come to Hawai'i. In 1809, young 'Ōpūkahai'a swam from the beach at Nāpo'opo'o to the safety of Captain Britnall's

American ship anchored in Kealakekua Bay. Defying his uncle, who was training him for the priesthood near Hikiau Heiau, ʻŌpūkahaiʻa chose to travel to the United States. Once in New England, his conversion to Christianity inspired him with a desire to return to Hawaiʻi as a missionary and share his new faith with his own people. Unfortunately, he died of typhus fever in Connecticut at the age of twenty-six before his dream could be realized.

The remains of ʻŌpūkahaiʻa's body were moved to Kahikolu Church in 1993. The entrance to Kahikolu Church is marked by a sign on the *makai* side of Nāpoʻopoʻo Road. Follow the gravel road to the church parking lot. (14/38; 5/61)

35. Kealakekua Bay Archaeological and Historical District

Thousands of Hawaiians once lived in small villages along the shores and hillsides surrounding Kealakekua Bay. Fishing, surfing, swimming, and canoe paddling filled the protected waters of the bay with activity. Cultivated upland garden plots, within easy walking distance of the shore, supplied residents with food and materials for clothing. Religious and ceremonial life was centered around Hikiau Heiau where *kāhuna* and *aliʻi* fulfilled their ritual duties.

In 1779, this world changed forever with the arrival of Captain James Cook. Once news of the existence of the Sandwich Islands reached Europe, explorers and traders sailed to Kealakekua Bay in increasing numbers. By 1820, ships carrying cargoes of California cattle, sea otter furs, and whale oil had dropped anchor off Kaʻawaloa, the principal village on the northern side of the bay. Hawaiians had no way to cope with the introduction of European diseases and intoxicating alcohol that accompanied these encounters. At times, their culture appeared to be at a disadvantage compared to the newcomers' wealth and power. The apparent superiority of iron over stone, of guns over wooden spears, of woven cloth over *kapa* (*tapa* or bark cloth), of the Christian god over the Hawaiian gods, and of English ships over canoes was overwhelming. The wave of change which washed over Hawaiʻi was generated in these waters.

The State of Hawaiʻi plans to create a historical park at Kealakekua Bay to tell the stories associated with this important and scenic area. Even the rugged rock face of this *pali* (cliff) conceals a part of Hawaiʻi's past. The *pali* is riddled with lava tubes, many of them used by ancient Hawaiians as burial caves for the remains of their *aliʻi*. (10/9)

35A. Hikiau Heiau

Tsunami and 19th century road building have demolished parts of the original stone platform, but in 1779, Hikiau Heiau stood prominently at the head of Kealakekua Bay. As ruling chief Kalaniʻōpuʻu's *luakini* or state *heiau*, it was a significant site. It was on these very stones that the priests of Lono brought Captain James Cook for religious ceremonies after his arrival. A monument commemmorating the first Christian burial in Hawaiʻi stands in front of the *heiau* today.

According to noted Hawaiian scholar, John Stokes, Hikiau Heiau was part of a much larger religious complex which included a sacred enclosure surrounded by stone walls, a sacred pool located inland from the beach, a house for *kāhuna*, and tiny Helehelekalani Heiau. When Stokes visited the site in 1906, modern structures such as a prison and a bullock pen had encroached on the property.

Although it seems impossible to imagine today, Nāpoʻopoʻo used to be a favorite cattle shipping beach frequently used by local ranchers from 1880 until 1928. Plus, as a spot for swimming, Nāpoʻopoʻo was perfect until 20th-century storms and tsunami transformed the sandy beach into the rock-strewn bank that is seen today. (8/115; 18/98-101)

35B. Captain Cook's Monument at Kaʻawaloa

The white obelisk at Kaʻawaloa commemorates Captain James Cook, England's brilliant explorer and navigator, who was killed here on February 14, 1779. After his death, his partial remains were buried at sea in Kealakekua Bay. In 1878, a few of Cook's "fellow countrymen" erected the monument standing today.

It was during Cook's third voyage of exploration, on January 18, 1778, that he first saw Oʻahu and Kauaʻi. He named them the "Sandwich Islands" in honor of the Earl of Sandwich, then First Lord

The *Resolution* and *Discovery* at Kealakekua Bay, ca. 1779.
Engraving after a drawing by John Webber.

of the British Admiralty, and Cook's friend and patron. After a two-weeks visit on Kaua'i and Ni'ihau, he sailed north to the Arctic in search of the "Northwest Passage." Unsuccessful, he returned to the Sandwich Islands in November of 1778 to escape the winter weather. Skirting the rocky coastlines of Maui and Hawai'i, he chose Kealakekua Bay as a safe refuge. As the *Resolution* and *Discovery* sailed into Kealakekua's blue waters, the English sailors on board were greeted by a flotilla of Hawaiians in canoes, offering gifts of food and words of welcome. Cook was greeted by Koa, the powerful priest of Lono, and treated like a visiting king, or, as some say, a visiting god. After a peaceful and pleasant visit, Cook left Kealakekua Bay, planning to return to the Arctic. A storm broke the *Resolution*'s foremast, forcing a return to Kealakekua Bay to repair the ship and re-supply the vessels with food and water.

Cook's second sojourn at Kealakekua Bay started calmly. However, after the theft of a small boat by the Hawaiians, Cook decided to bring Kalani'ōpu'u, the powerful but aging high chief, on board the *Resolution* as a hostage. Once the missing boat was returned, the chief would go free. Cook had used this strategy successfully elsewhere in Polynesia during his travels and expected no trouble.

While Cook was on shore at Ka'awaloa, attempting to persuade Kalani'ōpu'u to accompany him back to his ship, news reached the village that the English had shot a prominent chief. Cook decided to abandon his scheme and return to his ship. Unfortunately, fighting broke out before he and his marines could escape. In Captain King's account of Cook's death he wrote:

> Four of the marines were cut off amongst the rocks in their retreat, and fell as a sacrifice to the fury of the enemy; three more were dangerously wounded; and the Lieutenant, who had recieved a stab between the shoulders with a pahooa, having fortunately reserved his fire, shot the man who had wounded him just as he was going to repeat his blow. Our unfortunate Commander, the last time he was seen distinctly, was standing at the water's edge, and calling out to the boats to cease firing, and to pull in.

Was Cook actually asking his men to stop firing, or did he need the boats to come ashore because he could not swim? No one can say for certain, but Cook died on the rocks of Ka'awaloa. More Hawaiians died than British seamen in this unfortunate mishap. King wrote that seventeen Hawaiians were killed at Ka'awaloa, five of them chiefs. Eight died at the observatory near Hikiau Heiau in a subsequent fight.

The repercussions of that fateful encounter are felt even today.

H. Hackfeld & Co. Ltd. at Nāpo'opo'o Landing, ca. 1915.
(Courtesy Bishop Museum Archives)

A hero to some and a symbol of western imperialism to others, one fact remains: Cook died at this spot and his memory lingers. (3/277; 4/45, 81)

35C. Nāpoʻopoʻo Landing

The concrete wharf at Nāpoʻopoʻo is a reminder that this spot was a busy port and active commercial center from the late 1800s to the early 1900s. H. Hackfeld & Co. Ltd., prominant German agents and shippers for sugar plantations throughout the islands, built a large store next to the wharf in approximately 1900, which served local farmers and ranchers. Inter-island steamers visited this bay regularly, unloading supplies and mail, and picking up cattle, coffee, hides, butter, and local produce for Honolulu.

Once regular steamer service stopped, Nāpoʻopoʻo ceased to exist as a commercial center as residents died or moved away. The small stores that once sold milk and bread closed. H. Hackfeld & Co., by then American Factors, no longer had a commercial interest in South Kona. With better roads being built throughout Kona, Kailua Bay became the favorite port and the large old store crumbled into ruin.

36. Mokuʻōhai Battlefield

The ruling chief of Hawaiʻi, Kalaniʻōpuʻu, decided before his death in 1782 to leave his lands to his son, Kiwalaʻō. To his nephew, Kamehameha, he entrusted his war god, Kūkaʻilimoku. According to historian John Papa Iʻi, Kamehameha felt a deep respect for his older cousin Kiwalaʻō and had no wish to quarrel with his demands. However, when Kiwalaʻō's chiefs became greedy, Kamehameha and his allies felt war was the only solution.

The two factions met in battle at Mokuʻōhai, a rough lava field not far from Nāpoʻopoʻo, in mid-1782. According to Iʻi, after several days of skirmishing, Kiwalaʻō took the upper hand. He captured Keʻeaumoku, the ruling chief of Kona and Kamehameha's ally, and threatened to kill him. When news of this disaster reached Kamehameha, he hastened to Mokuʻōhai, accompanied by his future wife, Kaʻahumanu, daughter of Keʻeaumoku.

At that critical moment, one of Kamehameha's expert stone

throwers, Pahia, flung a stone at Kiwalaʻō, hitting him in the temple with such force that the chief fell to the ground. Kiwalaʻō had the bad luck to fall on or near Keʻeaumoku who took his enemy by the throat and slashed it with a *lei o mano* (shark-tooth knife), killing him.

Kamehameha won the battle of Mokuʻōhai, but his victory did not bring peace. Although Kiwalaʻō was vanquished, his uncle and younger brother escaped, regrouped their forces, and spent the next ten years fighting amongst each other and against Kamehameha for supremacy of the island of Hawaiʻi. (8/36)

37. Puʻuhonua o Hōnaunau (Place of Refuge)

Established as a National Historical Park in 1961, Puʻuhonua o Hōnaunau is Hawaiʻi's best preserved and most well known place of refuge. Located on South Kona's relatively untouched coastline, this prehistoric site has been restored to present an authentic picture of one aspect of life in ancient Hawaiʻi. Although no city ever existed at Hōnaunau, the famous sanctuary formerly was called "the city of refuge" after a supposed biblical counterpart.

In ancient Hawaiʻi, the penalty for breaking many laws was death. If a woman ate prohibited foods such as certain types of bananas or pork, she was killed. If a man allowed his shadow to fall upon a sacred chief or he mistakenly touched a chief's possessions, he was killed.

In a culture of harsh penalties, a remarkable safety valve existed, the *puʻuhonua* or place of refuge. At these designated places, a person could escape death by coming before the resident *kahuna* for a ceremony of absolution. Once the ceremony was complete, the offender could safely return to his home, confident that the gods were appeased. No one, not even the mightiest king, could harm a person after he or she had reached the *puʻuhonua*. In times of war, women, children and the infirm flocked to the *puʻuhonua* to escape death at the hands of marauding warriors.

A striking feature at Hōnaunau is the massive stone wall over 1,000 feet long which marked the landward boundary of the *puʻuhonua*. Imagine desperate people struggling to get within the safety of the wall to avoid death and punishment at the hands of warriors and priests. The restored royal complex of the mighty chief

ern end of the wall features the Hale o Keawe Heiau
carved replicas of images of ancient gods and rebuilt
s. One of these thatched houses represents Hale o
s mortuary house which up until 1829 contained the
wenty-three high-ranking chiefs.

bert Louis Stevenson wrote about Hōnaunau in

sure of the sanctuary was all paved with lava; scattered
mbered it in places; everywhere tall coco palms jutted
sures and drew shadows on the floor; a loud continuous
e near sea burdened the ear. These rude monumental
he thought of that life and death of which they stood
hrew me in a muse. There are times and places where
comes more vivid than the present, and the memory
he ear and eye. I have found it so in the presence of the
Rome; I found it so again in the city of refuge at
and the strange, busy, and perilous existence of the old
the grinning idols of the heiau, the priestly murderers
ting victim, rose before and mastered my imagination.

1, 138)

38. St. Benedict's Catholic Church (Painted Church)

A Roman Catholic church once stood at the shore of Hōnaunau. In 1900, it was rebuilt inland at Hōnaunau *mauka* where the majority of the Hawaiian congregation had moved to live. This is St. Benedict's Church, known as the Painted Church because of Father John Berchmans Velghe's skill with a paint brush.

Father Velghe arrived at Hōnaunau in 1899 at the age of 41. Born in Belgium, he was familiar with Polynesia having served as a priest in Tahiti and the Marquesas. Having painted Bible stories on church interiors in his former parishes, he chose to decorate St. Benedict's as well.

Thanks to his creative use of housepaint, the interior of St. Benedict's looks like a small cathedral. With painted palm fronds sprouting from the tops of brightly striped red and white columns, a vaulted ceiling spangled with stars, and detailed Biblical scenes lining the walls, the "painted church" is unique. The congregation must have been amazed.

In 1902, Father Velghe painted the inside walls of Maria Lanakila (Mary the Victorious) at the coastal village of Kealia near Ho'okena. That church was destroyed in the 1951 earthquake. Velghe was called back to Belgium in 1904 where he continued to teach and paint throughout Europe until shortly before his death in 1939.

In 1924, Father John trained a young Belgian student named Matthias Gielen, who later became Father Evarist. Father Evarist created this island's two other "painted churches" at Kalapana and Mountain View, inspired, no doubt, by his former teacher.

39. Hōnaunau Japanese Language School (SKEA)

Built around 1900, this wooden building housed the Hōnaunau Nihongo Gakko or local Japanese language school until the onset of World War II in Hawai'i. Although the school was reopened after the war, it fell into disrepair and was closed. It was thanks to a grassroots community effort in the 1970s that the building was rescued, repaired, and restored to the community.

In 1981, the South Kona Education Association (SKEA) was founded. As a community organization committed to arts education for Kona's students, it has utilized the old language school as its headquarters.

Like the first missionaries who built their churches from the ruins of *heiau*, newcomers continue to adapt old structures to suit new purposes.

40. Ho'okena Village

Ho'okena was once a vibrant 19th century port town rivalled only by Kailua in size and importance. Tsunami, a drastic drop in the Hawaiian population, and the end of inter-island steamship travel have combined to erase almost all trace of Ho'okena's colorful past. In the 1880s, Ho'okena contained a school, two churches, two stores, a sturdy wharf, a courthouse built in 1884, and a fine cluster of well-built homes.

Queen Lili'uokalani decribed Ho'okena in 1881 as being distinctly Hawaiian. In 1890, Whitney's tourist guide said, "Ho'okena is . . . probably the last specimen on the islands of a purely Hawaiian community." Ho'okena attracted author Robert Louis Stevenson who visited in 1889 and stayed for a week. His host was Mr. Nahinu, a former judge and, at that time, storekeeper for Henry Cooper. (The Hawaiian song "Kupa's Landing" refers to Cooper's store at Ho'okena.) Stevenson's *Travels in Hawaii* includes a story about a young Hawaiian girl and her mother being transported from Ho'okena to Moloka'i's leper settlement at Kalaupapa.

By the 1890s, Chinese immigrants moved into town. Licenses issued included those for cake peddling, selling food and merchandise, running a retail store, butchering pork, and operating two restaurants and a hotel. In 1915, the Hilo newspaper reported that the community held a Fourth of July celebration attended by 500 Kona citizens featuring canoe races and a big *lu'au* (feast).

By 1929, the wharf was receiving freight only twice a month, so the stores and post office had closed.

During World War II, soldiers stationed nearby amused themselves by shooting at a colony of seabirds which nested in the lava cliffs above the beach. The birds never recovered. Between the termites

Ho'okena Village, ca. 1890. (Courtesy KHS Archives)

and the earthquake of 1951, both Puka'ana Church (1855) and Maria Lanakila (1860s) collapsed into ruin. A hike along the coast from the county park at Ho'okena to the north will reveal traces of old Ho'okena: stone house platforms, church ruins, and fragments of the old wharf. (1/25)

41. Ho'ōpūloa Flow of 1926

Ho'ōpūloa was once a small Hawaiian fishing village located just north of Miloli'i on the South Kona coast. Far from any good road, transportation to and from Ho'ōpūloa was easiest by canoe, and later, by steamer. An old donkey trail from the forest lands to the shoreline was used in the late 1800s by C.Q. Yee Hop Co. to haul large koa timbers to the Ho'ōpūloa landing for shipment to Honolulu. This trail was probably a footpath formerly used by Hawaiians to walk to their upland taro patches. Mail and supplies were landed on a regular basis, linking this isolated spot to the rest of the world.

In 1926, the red glare of an eruption from Mauna Loa's southwest rift zone warned residents a lava flow was heading their

Lava flow overtakes the village of Ho'ōpūloa, 18 April 1926. Photograph by Tai Sing Loo. (Courtesy KHS Archives)

way. The American Red Cross came to the rescue by canoe, paddling frantic residents and their possessions to safety at nearby Miloli'i. As the lava rolled into the sea, dead fish bobbed to the surface for miles around, boiled to death by the lava-heated water. The village of Ho'ōpūloa was completely destroyed.

From Kīholo to Ho'ōpūloa, Pele's fires have brought a mixed blessing to Kona. New land for future generations to settle and cultivate comes at a high price—total devastation of familiar and fruitful lands. However, early Hawaiians learned how to endure lava flows, tsunami, and earthquakes hundreds of years ago.

42. Miloli'i

Miloli'i is a small coastal village near the southern boundary of the Kona district. Once known for its excellent sennit (twisted coconut fiber twine or rope), it is now known as a Hawaiian fishing village whose residents prize their privacy and independence.

Hawaiian fishermen at Ke'ei, South Kona, ca. 1970. Photograph by Norman K. Carlson. (Courtesy KHS Archives)

Glossary of Some Hawaiian Terms

ahupua'a   Land division running from the sea to the uplands. Boundaries were marked by an ahu (heap) of stones surmounted by an image of a pig (pua'a).

ali'i   Chief, chiefess, king, queen, royalty, nobility, high born.

'aumakua   Family or personal god.

haole   A white person, American, English: formerly, any foreigner.

heiau   Hawaiian temple, place of worship or offering, stone platform, walled enclosure or terrace.

hōlua   The sled course, and especially the ancient sled used on grassy slopes. Papa hōlua, sled.

kahuna   Priest, minister, sorcerer, expert in any profession.

kai   Sea, sea water: current in the sea.

kapu   Taboo, forbidden, sacred, consecrated.

koa   Native forest tree (*Acacia koa*).

Kona   Leeward sides of the Hawaiian Islands.

Kū   One of the four great gods, best known as a god of war.

Kūka'ilimoku   The most famous of the Kū war images owned by Kamehameha I. Literal meaning is Kū island-snatcher.

lei   Flower or leafy garland for head or neck.

lei o mano   A weapon, a large shark tooth set in a piece of wood about two and a half inches long, with a string loop for attaching to the finger.

Lono One of the four great gods, considered a god of clouds, winds, the sea, agriculture, and fertility. He was the patron of the annual harvest Makahiki festivals.

luakini Hawaiian temple where ruling chiefs prayed and human sacrifices were offered.

Makahiki Ancient festival beginning in late-October with the rising of the Pleiades and lasting up to four months. Sport and religious festivities are conducted at this time and war is forbidden.

makai Toward the ocean.

mana Supernatural or divine power.

mauka Inland, upland, toward the mountains.

mauna Mountain, mountainous region.

Menehune Legendary race of people who worked at night during prehistoric times building fishponds, roads, and temples.

pāhoa Short dagger; sharp stone, especially as used for a weapon.

paniolo Hawaiian cowboy.

Pele Volcano goddess.

poi The Hawaiian staff of life, made from cooked taro corms, pounded and thinned with water.

puʻu Any kind of protuberance from a pimple to a hill, bulge, heap, peak, or mound.

puʻuhonua Place of refuge, sanctuary.

waʻa Canoe.

wai Fresh water, any liquid other than sea water.

World Events Time Line		Hawaiian Time Line	
Fall of the Roman Empire	500 A.D.	0 - 900 A.D.	First Polynesian settlers arrive in Hawai'i
Vikings sail to Iceland	700		
Aztecs in Mexico	1200		
Christopher Columbus discovers "New World"	1492		
		1527	Possible shipwrecked Spaniards land at Ke'ei
Magellan sails around the world	1519- 1522		
Pilgrims arrive in America	1620	c. 1758	Kamehameha the Great born in North Kohala
U.S. Declaration of Independence	1776	1778	Captain James Cook arrives in Hawai'i
		1779	Death of Captain Cook at Kealakekua Bay *page 58*
		1782	Battle of Moku'ōhai *page 61*
		1793- 1794	First cattle landed at Kealakekua Bay *page 20*
		1795	Kamehameha's victory at Battle of Nu'uanu leads to unification of Hawaiian Kingdom
		1801	Hualālai erupts *page 10*
		1803	First horses landed at Kawaihae, S. Kohala
		1809	'Ōpūkahai'a sails to New England *page 56*
Napoleon invades Russia	1812	1812	Kamehameha returns to Kona Sandalwood trade is royal monopoly
		1814	Birth of Kauikeauoli at Keauhou *page 36*
		1819	Kamehameha I dies; his son Liholiho becomes Kamehameha II *page 24*
		1819	Battle of Kuamo'o; old order destroyed *page 37* First whale ships arrive in islands
		1820	New England missionaries arrive in Kailua
		1824	Liholiho dies of measles in England
		1825	Kauikeauoli becomes king Kamehameha III *page 36*
		1827	First Catholic missionaries in Hawai'i
		1828	First coffee planted in Kona
		1837	Moku'aikaua Church dedicated in Kailua, Kona *page 25*
Victoria crowned Queen of England	1838	1838	Hulihe'e Palace completed *page 27*
California "Gold Rush"	1848	1845- 1850	The Mahele allows land ownership
Livingstone's first African journey	1849	1852	Chinese imported for plantation labor
		1853	First smallpox epidemic
American Civil War	1861- 1865	1867	First Anglican church built in Kona *page 50*

Telephone invented	1876	1868	First Japanese immigrants in Hawai'i Kaona Uprising *page 43*
		1873	Author Isabella Bird tours Hawai'i *page 11*
		1878	First Portuguese immigrants arrive
		1893	Queen Lili'uokalani overthrown
		1894	Republic of Hawai'i established
		1898	Hawai'i annexed to the United States Kona Sugar Co. established
		1899	Kona Railroad begun for sugar *page 18*
Wright brothers' first flight	1903	1903	First "horseless buggy" in Kona
Panama Canal completed - first cargo to pass through is a bargeload of sugar from Hawai'i	1914		
World War I	1914- 1918		
Worldwide Spanish flu epidemic	1919	1919	Spanish flu epidemic in Kona
		1924	Major sugar strike in Hawai'i Filipino laborers move to Kona
		1928	Kona Inn opens *page 28*
		1929	Major earthquake in Kona
		1932	Over 1,000 coffee farms in Kona Public school "coffee schedule" starts
Amelia Earhart makes first solo flight between Hawai'i and the mainland	1935	1934	First modern Hawaiian canoe races
World War II	1939- 1945	1941- 1945	World War II in the Pacific
		1949	First Honolulu to Kona commercial flight
		1951	Kona's heaviest recorded earthquake
		1959	Statehood for Hawai'i International Billfish Tournament begins
		1960	Original King Kamehameha Hotel built at Kamakahonu
President J.F. Kennedy assassinated	1963	1967	One million tourists visit Hawai'i Nine hole golf course opens in Keauhou
First man on the moon	1969	1969	End of "coffee schedule" in Kona schools
		1970	Kona International Airport completed
American Bicentennial	1976	1976	*Hokule'a* sails to Tahiti
		1983	Current eruption starts at Kīlauea
		1985	100th anniversary of Kanyaku Japanese arrival in Hawai'i
		1986	Ellison Onizuka killed in *Challenger* explosion *page 14*
		1993	100th anniversary of the overthrow of the Kingdom of Hawai'i
			200th anniversary of first cattle landing at Kealakekua Bay

Bibliography

1.   *A Plan for Kona.* Prepared for the Hawaii State Planning Office by Harland Bartholomew and Associates. Honolulu: May, 1960.

2.   Barrère, Dorothy B. "Kamehameha in Kona: Two Documentary Studies." *Pacific Anthropological Records No. 23.* Honolulu: Bernice P. Bishop Museum, 1975.

3.   Bird, Isabella L. *Six Months Among the Palm Groves, Coral Reefs and Volcanoes of the Sandwich Islands.* London: John Murray, 1890. Tokyo: Charles E. Tuttle Company, 1990.

4.   Cook, James and James King. *A Voyage to the Pacific Ocean . . . in His Majesty's Ships* Resolution *and* Discovery. 3 vols. and an atlas of plates. London: H. Hughs, 1785.

5.   Daws, Gavan. *Shoal of Time: A History of the Hawaiian Islands.* New York: Macmillan, 1968; Honolulu: University Press of Hawaii, 1974.

6.   Day, A. Grove. *History Makers of Hawaii.* Honolulu: Mutual Publishing of Honolulu, 1984.

7.   Ellis, Reverend William. *A Narrative of a Tour Through Hawaii in 1823.* Honolulu: Hawaiian Gazette Co., Ltd., 1917

8.   I'i, John Papa. *Fragments of Hawaiian History.* Honolulu: Bishop Museum Press, 1959.

9.   Kamakau, Samuel M. *Ruling Chiefs of Hawaii,* Revised Edition. Honolulu: The Kamehameha Schools Press, 1992.

10.   Kelly, Marion. *Na Mala O Kona: Gardens of Kona, A History of Land Use in Kona, Hawai'i.* Department of Anthropology, Bernice P. Bishop Museum. Honolulu, Hawai'i, 1983.

11.   Kona Historical Society. *Important Dates in Kona's Past.*

12.   Loucks, Ruth C. *Commissioned to Hawaii, The Life of Albert S. Baker.* Seattle: Published by Carol Higgins, 1978.

13.   Malo, David. *Hawaiian Antiquities.* Translated by Nathaniel B. Emerson. Honolulu: Gazette, 1903, 1951, 1971.

14.   Paris, The Rev. John D. *Fragments of a Real Missionary Life.* Published by "The Friend." Honolulu: 1926.

15.   Pukui, Mary K., and Samuel H. Elbert. *Hawaiian Dictionary.* Honolulu: University Press of Hawaii, 1977.

16.   Pukui, Mary K., Samuel H. Elbert, and Esther T. Mookini. *Place Names of Hawaii.* Honolulu: The University Press of Hawaii, 1974.

17.   Stevenson, Robert Louis. *Travels in Hawaii.* Edited by A. Grove Day. Honolulu: University of Hawaii Press, 1991.

18.   Stokes, John F.G. *Heiau on the Island of Hawai'i: A Historic Survey of Native Hawaiian Temple Sites.* Honolulu: Bishop Museum Press, 1991.